TOP **10**
NEW ORLEANS

Top 10 New Orleans Highlights

The Top 10 of Everything

CONTENTS

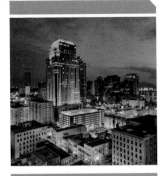

New Orleans Area by Area

Streetsmart

Within each Top 10 list in this book, no hierarchy of quality or popularity is implied. All 10 are, in the editor's opinion, of roughly equal merit.

Throughout this book, floors are referred to in accordance with American usage; i.e., the "first floor" is at ground level.

Title page, front cover, and spine *The lively Bourbon Street in the French Quarter*
Back cover, clockwise from top left *Old houses, French Quarter; Streetcars in Lousiana; Crescent City Connection Bridge; Royal Street, French Quarter; Jackson Square*

The rate at which the world is changing is constantly keeping the DK Eyewitness team on our toes. While we've worked hard to ensure that this edition of New Orleans is accurate and up-to-date, we know that opening hours alter, standards shift, prices fluctuate, places close and new ones pop up in their stead. So, if you notice we've got something wrong or left something out, we want to hear about it. Please get in touch at **travelguides@dk.com**

Welcome to
New Orleans

The Crescent City. Birthplace of jazz and home to delicious Creole, Cajun, and Southern food. Wrought-iron railings, lively Mardi Gras, and rumbling streetcars. Voodoo and atmospheric cemeteries. Street musicians and parades. New Orleans is a small city with a huge reputation. With DK Eyewitness Top 10 New Orleans, it's yours to explore.

Located at the mouth of the mighty **Mississippi River**, a busy commercial waterway, New Orleans has a rich history. Here, French and Spanish influences blend with the Cajun and Creole flavors of Africa and the Caribbean. With its iron filigree balconies and centuries-old houses, the historic **French Quarter** is a living movie set, while the leafier environs of the **Garden District** house postcard-perfect Southern mansions. Stroll along the river or ride the streetcars for evocative tours of the neighborhoods.

New Orleans' passion for the good life is obvious everywhere you walk, from its fine-dining restaurants to the street musicians' jazz soundtrack. Traffic often stops for **daily parades**, which mark everything from weddings to funerals, and the exuberant **Mardi Gras** celebrations when the biggest street party extravaganza takes over the city for a month every year.

Whether you're visiting for a weekend or a week, our Top 10 guide brings together the best of everything New Orleans has to offer, from beautiful green spaces such as **City Park** and infamous city hangouts such as **Bourbon Street**, to **jazz clubs** with the best local musicians, and testaments to history such as **The National World War II Museum**. Whether it's seeking out what's free or just avoiding the crowds, the guide has useful tips throughout, plus seven easy-to-follow itineraries designed to tie together a clutch of sights in a short space of time. Add inspiring photography and detailed maps, and you've got the essential pocket-sized travel companion. **Enjoy the book and enjoy New Orleans.**

Clockwise from top: French Quarter buildings, the modern skyline, St. Mary's Assumption Church, jazz performers in the French Quarter, Botanical Garden, a Mardi Gras costume

Exploring New Orleans

New Orleans is one of the most interesting cities in the U.S., with historic neighborhoods dating back 300 years. There's a lot to take in, so here are some ideas for a two- and four-day city adventure. The real beauty is that you can enjoy the best New Orleans has to offer by just walking around.

The Mississippi Riverfront, with its steamboats, is a great starting point for exploring the city.

Two Days in New Orleans

Day ❶

MORNING

Start with a walk past the steamboats and riverside lawns on the **Mississippi Riverfront** (see pp22–3), then head to **The Historic New Orleans Collection** (see pp20–21) to learn about the past of this uniquely Caribbean–European–American city.

AFTERNOON

After crossing **Canal Street** (see pp36–7), head into the Warehouse District to spend a while wandering around the enormous exhibits of **The National World War II Museum** (see pp18–19). Then take the streetcar uptown and enjoy a walk around the sprawling **Audubon Park** (see p73).

Day ❷

MORNING

You can take your time admiring the diverse exhibits in the **New Orleans Museum of Art** (see pp12–15), and visiting the adjoining Sculpture Garden. Stop at the Morning Call Coffee Stand before embarking on a walking or biking tour of **New Orleans City Park** (see pp16–17).

AFTERNOON

Head downtown and buy some local art at **Jackson Square** (see pp26–7), before browsing the galleries and antiques stores of **Royal Street** (see pp28–31). When you've finished, **Bourbon Street** (see pp32–3) should be starting to get lively.

Four Days in New Orleans

Day ❶

MORNING

Start your day downtown, with the sights around **Jackson Square** (see pp26–7) and the **Mississippi Riverfront** (see pp22–3), including the historic **French Market** (see p90).

AFTERNOON

You can meander toward **Canal Street** (see pp36–7) via the antiques shops and art collections on **Royal Street** (see pp28–31) before making your way back down **Bourbon Street** (see pp32–3) for world-class jazz clubs.

CARROLLTON

UNIVERSITY DISTRICT

STREETCAR

Audubon Park

0 km   1
0 miles   1

Audubon Park is an oasis of fountains and ponds fringed by tropical foliage.

The imposing St. Louis Cathedral is the centerpiece of New Orleans' historic park, Jackson Square.

Key
— Two-day itinerary
— Four-day itinerary

The **Louis Armstrong Park** is perfect for a morning stroll.

Day ❷
MORNING
Make it a day appreciating the wildlife of New Orleans. Start by taking a stroll through the vast **Audubon Park** (see p73), looking out for egrets and heron around Bird Island, in the center of the park's lagoon.
AFTERNOON
To see more Louisiana wildlife, head out to the swamplands south of the city by boat on one of the **Jean Lafitte Swamp Tours** (see p48). You'll spot alligators, deer, and many birds.

Day ❸
MORNING
Rent a bicycle and ride around the landscaped greenery of **New Orleans City Park** (see pp16–17), stopping only to wander around the **New Orleans Museum of Art** (see pp12–15).
AFTERNOON
Stroll along **Decatur Street** (see p90), stopping off for food and drinks, before jazz club-hopping your way up **Frenchmen Street** (see p96).

Day ❹
MORNING
Explore **Louis Armstrong Park** (see p97), before a lunch break in Treme.
AFTERNOON
Sunset brings out the colors of the houses in the Marigny and Bywater areas, and there's time to see the city skyline from **Crescent Park** (see p98) before dinner.

Top 10 New Orleans Highlights

St. Louis Cathedral, the centerpiece
of New Orleans' Jackson Square

New Orleans Highlights

New Orleans winds gracefully around a bend in the Mississippi River. The city has a rich multicultural history, evident in its food, architecture, and customs. Famous for its carefree vibe, New Orleans is also known for its jazz heritage, colorful festivities, and unmatched joie de vivre.

New Orleans Museum of Art

1

Founded in 1911 by Isaac Delgado, a sugar broker, the New Orleans Museum of Art has a collection of more than 40,000 artworks in 46 galleries, plus a lovely outdoor sculpture garden (see pp12–15).

New Orleans City Park

2

This park is New Orleans' version of Central Park in New York. A lush, landscaped space with dozens of attractions, it is a popular getaway from the urban bustle (see pp16–17).

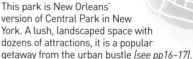

The National World War II Museum

3

This vast military history museum focuses on the American experience in World War II (see pp18–19).

The Historic New Orleans Collection

4

With an extensive array of maps and artifacts, this fascinating museum digs deep into the history of New Orleans (see pp20–21).

Mississippi Riverfront

5

New Orleans is bordered by the Mississippi. Take a streetcar ride alongside it, dine by the river, or board a steamboat for a cruise (see pp22–3).

Jackson Square **6**

Set in the center of the French Quarter, against the backdrop of St. Louis Cathedral, the attractive Jackson Square is surrounded by beautiful architecture *(see pp26–7)*.

7 Royal Street

One of the most beautiful streets in New Orleans, Royal Street offers the city's best fine art galleries, as well as antiques shops and great restaurants *(see pp28–31)*.

8 Bourbon Street

The ever-bustling Bourbon Street features some of the French Quarter's main attractions, including beautiful hotels, excellent vintage bars and restaurants, and plenty of live jazz. This street is a must-see for visitors *(see pp32–3)*.

Mardi Gras **9**

Billed as the world's largest street party, Mardi Gras is an annual spring celebration that culminates on Fat Tuesday (just before Lent). This festival, associated with feasting and parties, marks the last celebration before Lent *(see pp34–5)*.

10 Canal Street

Ride the streetcar, enjoy an outdoor lunch, shop at fine boutiques, or try your luck at Harrah's New Orleans Casino on one of the widest boulevards in the world *(see pp36–7)*.

TOP 10 ★ New Orleans Museum of Art

The city's oldest fine arts institution, and a historic landmark, the New Orleans Museum of Art, or NOMA, is one of the most important and comprehensive art museums in the Gulf South. This popular art repository displays works from the Renaissance to the modern era and is the centerpiece of the elegant New Orleans City Park. Its permanent collections and rotating exhibits rival the best museums in the country. NOMA is also a cultural center, hosting high-profile lectures, educational programs, films, and festivals.

1 NOMA Photography Collection

The museum has over 13,000 images featuring some of the greatest achievements within the medium. The great photography displayed here includes works by Diane Arbus, Ansel Adams, Man Ray, and Clarence John Laughlin.

2 Friday Nights at NOMA

On select Fridays, NOMA hosts special events (**above**) from 6pm. These include visiting exhibitions, lectures, film screenings, hands-on art workshops, family-friendly activities, and live performances.

3 Children's Events

NOMA makes every effort to be a fine arts museum that serves families as well as art aficionados. If you're traveling with children, check out their website for an events schedule that invariably includes creative workshops that are brilliant for artsy young travelers.

4 Museum Shop

No trip to NOMA is complete without a visit to the Museum Shop. It stocks products such as glass art, prints, books, and jewelry, among other things. It also showcases works by local artists.

5 The Annual Odyssey Ball

The premier event on the city's social calendar, the annual Odyssey Ball takes place in November. On this day, the museum is beautifully decorated and features auctions, an orchestra, and dancing.

6 Modern Art

This display covers the major movements in 20th-century European and American art. The pieces by Andy Warhol are highlights. There are contemporary works too.

THE BUILDING

Most visitors to NOMA are as dazzled by the building as they are by the exhibits inside. The Neo-Classical architecture of the original structure dates back to 1910. It was a gift from sugar broker Isaac Delgado, who envisioned a "temple of art for the rich and poor alike." Wings added in the 1990s complement the original structure, while seamlessly integrating into the surrounding natural environment.

7 Café NOMA

The museum café **(left)** is a sleek, atmospheric venue with floor-to-ceiling windows offering views over City Park. It was opened by New Orleans restaurant legend Ralph Brennan. The menu features a range of dishes prepared with fresh, seasonal ingredients supplied by local farmers.

NEED TO KNOW

MAP H2 ▪ 1 Collins Diboll Circle, New Orleans City Park ▪ 504-488-2631 ▪ www.noma.org

Open 10am–5pm Tue–Sat ▪ Adm $12 ($10 for seniors and students, $8 for children)

Sydney & Walda Besthoff Sculpture Garden: open 10am–6pm daily

▪ Take the Canal streetcar to City Park's main entrance, and walk down the grand promenade to NOMA.

▪ Just outside NOMA, Morning Call Café serves *café au lait* (French coffee) and *beignets* (pastries with powdered sugar).

Facade of NOMA

9 Special Exhibitions

In the past, NOMA showcased traveling exhibitions ranging from multimedia works by local and international artists to the Treasures of Ancient Egypt.

8 Sydney and Walda Besthoff Sculpture Garden

Beautifully landscaped, this garden features an outdoor collection of more than 90 sculptures **(right)**, most of which were donated by the Besthoff Foundation. A 6-acre (2.4-hectare) expansion in 2019 added an open-air amphitheater, pedestrian bridges, and a new gallery wing to the existing garden.

10 Wellness Classes in the Sculpture Garden

The garden is a great place for yoga classes, held on select Saturdays.

Floor Plan of NOMA
Key to Floor Plan
▪ First floor
▪ Second floor
▪ Third floor

Further Features of NOMA

An Italian Renaissance altarpiece in the European Art collection

1 European Art
French, Italian, Dutch, Flemish, and Impressionist works are showcased in the European Art section. The highlight is a wealth of Italian paintings from the Renaissance to the 18th century. The French collection includes a series of landscape paintings.

2 Louisiana Art
The galleries and period rooms along the mezzanine offer works of art created from the early 19th century in Louisiana. Works by internationally renowned sculptors such as John Scott and Lin Emery can be found in the courtyard and Sculpture Garden.

3 Public Programs
Every Friday the museum remains open until 9pm for special tours, performances, live music, screenings, and interactive workshops.

Artifact from Art of the Americas

4 African Art
This collection is considered one of the most important of its kind in American art museums. It features figures, sculptures, ancient terracottas, textiles, furniture, masks, costumes, marionettes, and musical instruments.

5 Asian Art
NOMA began its collection of Asian art in 1914 with a selection of Chinese jade and stone carvings. Today there are Chinese ceramics, Japanese Edo-period (1603–1868) paintings, and Indian art.

6 Oceanic Art
Indigenous art from Polynesia, Indonesia, and Melanesia is at the forefront of this collection from the Oceania region. Do not miss rare pieces from Borneo and the Nias Islands, as well as the fine cotton ritual weavings from Sumatra.

7 Art of the Americas
North, Central, and South American art are the focus here, with works ranging from Mayan artifacts to pre-Columbian artworks, right through to the Spanish colonial period. The section also includes a collection of art by Indigenous communities, dating from ancient times to the present day, and a selection of Louisiana paintings.

8 Decorative Art
More than 15,000 works comprise this distinctive collection, which covers glass art, American

art pottery, French ceramics, miniature portraits, and furniture. Also on display is a wall-mounted collection of seminal chair designs by Ray and Charles Eames.

9 Photography, Prints, and Drawings

These rotating collections consist of more than 20,000 objects including prints, books, and unique works on paper that are displayed in a special suite of galleries. This particular department has two exhibitions a year. Highlights of the exhibits include works by French artist Henri Matisse.

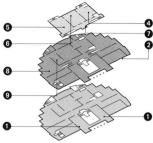

Further Features of NOMA

10 Scavenger Hunts

Free scavenger hunts at the Sydney and Walda Besthoff Sculpture Garden (see p104) are very popular.

PERMANENT EXHIBITS

NOMA's permanent collection includes more than 40,000 artworks from all over the world. Among the highlights are rare pieces from the Americas, Asia, and Europe. The collection continues to grow with new acquisitions. Art aficionados will probably notice the preponderance of French and American art.

This portrait of Marie Antoinette was painted by Élisabeth Louise Vigée Le Brun in 1788.

TOP 10 HIGHLIGHTS

1 Élisabeth Louise Vigée Le Brun's portrait of Marie Antoinette, Queen of France

2 William-Adolphe Bouguereau's painting *Whisperings of Love*

3 Alfred Boisseu's *Louisiana Indians Walking Along a Bayou*

4 Edgar Degas' portrait of Estelle Musson Degas

5 J. S. Copley's *Portrait of Colonel George Watson*

6 A well-curated collection of 18th- and 19th-century housewares, decor, and furniture from across the U.S.

7 *Death Comes to the Banquet Table* by Giovanni Martinelli

8 Chinese jade and hardstone carvings donated by the Morgan-Whitney family

9 *Portrait of Mrs. Asher B. Wertheimer* by John Singer Sargent

10 A vast glass collection, from Ancient Egypt to contemporary creations

TOP 10 ★ New Orleans City Park

Built on the site of the former Allard Plantation beside Bayou St. John, New Orleans City Park is one of the biggest urban parks in the country. A perfect spot for children and adults alike, it offers sports facilities, museums, waterways, golf courses, an amusement park, a miniature golf course, a botanical garden, and much more. The park is also home to the New Orleans Museum of Art and the Sydney and Walda Besthoff Sculpture Garden, which showcases over 60 modern sculptures.

New Orleans Botanical Garden **1**

Botanical exhibits and themed gardens – including the famous rose gardens – cover 10 acres (4 ha) of this park **(right)**. Sculptures by artist Enrique Alférez stand among the trees.

2 Old Oak Grove

New Orleans is home to the world's largest grove of mature oaks **(below)**. The oldest tree here is believed to be over 800 years old.

3 Louisiana Children's Museum

Interactive displays as well as exhibits are the focus of this family-friendly museum *(see p45)*. It has been relocated from the Warehouse District.

NEED TO KNOW
MAP H1 ■ 504-482-4888
■ Canal St streetcar
■ www.neworleanscity
park.com
New Orleans Botanical Garden: open 10am–4:30pm Tue–Thu & Sun (to 4pm Fri & Sat); adm
Louisiana Children's Museum: 15 Henry Thomas Dr; open 9:30am–4:30pm Wed–Sat, 11:30am–4:30pm Sun; adm

Carousel Gardens Amusement Park: 1 Palm Dr; open 11am–6pm Sat & Sun; adm

Train Garden: trains run 10am–4:30pm Sat & Sun; adm

Storyland: 504-483-9402; open 10am–Thu & Sun (to 3:30pm Fri & Sat); adm

■ The park may seem overwhelming to first-time visitors. You can download a map of the park from the website. Seasonal timings and prices vary; check the website for more details.

Carousel Gardens Amusement Park (4)

Featuring one of the last 100 antique carousels in the country, this amusement park has charmed visitors for over a century. It also includes a dozen other rides, which make the place a children's wonderland **(right)**.

Storyland (7)

This fairytale playground, with more than 20 exhibits from storybooks, is a major attraction for families. It is an ideal setting for children's parties.

Celebration in the Oaks (8)

The park is adorned with decorations and state-of-the-art lighting from Thanksgiving to New Year's Day. This is a favorite stop on most walking tours.

NOLA CITY BARK

Dog lovers visit City Park all the time, so the park officials created an entire section just for canines called "NOLA City Bark," entered from Magnolia Drive. It has separate facilities for large and small dogs, and those who bring their animals here must subscribe to the annual membership. The park is dotted with shaded areas and flowering trees, and even has a dog wash for messy animals.

Map of New Orleans City Park

Pavilion of the Two Sisters (5)

The semicircular pavilion is built in the style of a traditional European orangery and has become a very popular venue for receptions and fund-raisers, as well as other social events.

City Park/ Pepsi Tennis Center (9)

With 16 hard and 10 clay courts, this facility offers the best public tennis courts in the state of Louisiana. Visitors can rent equipment, but it is best to book in advance.

City Park Golf Courses (10)

A putter's heaven, City Park has two 18-hole golf courses. A championship-level course opened in 2017, featuring historic oak trees and lagoons characteristic of the park.

Train Garden (6)

A unique attraction tucked away in the vibrant Botanical Garden is a working miniature-train garden **(right)**, elevated to eye level. It features re-creations of the architectural structures and historic neighborhoods of New Orleans.

The National World War II Museum

The National World War II Museum is dedicated to interpreting the country's contribution to the largest armed conflict in history. It features newsreels, artifacts, movies, and interactive displays that re-create bunkers, ship bridges, and even battlefields. Especially fascinating are the two Campaigns of Courage pavilions, which tell personal stories of American service members from the war.

1 Desert War: North Africa

This large re-creation (**above**) of the Tunisian desert includes projected images of tanks rumbling over sand next to a 1943 jeep and a howitzer. An artifact case displays the weapons used during the North African campaign.

2 BB's Stage Door Canteen

Located in the Solomon Victory Theater, this zone re-creates live entertainment that was used to sustain morale during the war. The bill includes 1940s-era stage shows; the Victory Belles vocal trio is especially popular.

3 The Arsenal of Democracy

An entire wing (**below**) of the museum is devoted to exploring the causes of World War II, its impact on civilian life, and the social divisions – such as racial inequity – that plagued the USA before, during, and after the war.

THE HIGGINS BOAT

New Orleans was chosen as the location of The National World War II Museum because of the Higgins Boat, the iconic landing craft used at Normandy and multiple other World War II operations. The boat was designed in Louisiana, modified from the shallow draft vessels used in local wetlands. The re-created Higgins Boat and information on the craft can be found in the Louisiana Memorial Pavilion of the museum.

4 Beyond All Boundaries

A multimedia epic, this 45-minute 4D movie is presented in the Solomon Victory Theater. It is narrated by actor Tom Hanks and offers a truly immersive experience – "snow" falls, seats shake, and the audience finds itself misted with fog.

7 Guadalcanal: Green Hell

This exhibit on the 1942 Battle of Guadalcanal is set within an artificial Pacific island jungle. On display are the uniforms and arms of the U.S. and Japanese forces, giving an insight into how the battle was fought on land, sea, and air.

10 Final Mission

Set within the U.S. Freedom Pavilion, this exhibit **(above)** is almost like a theme park attraction. It tells the story of the final mission of the submarine USS *Tang*. Visitors take on the role of historical submarine crew within the re-created interior of the ill-fated naval vessel.

NEED TO KNOW

MAP Q3 ■ 945 Magazine St ■ 504-528-1944 ■ www.national ww2museum.org

Open 9am–5pm daily

Adm $32.50 for adults, $20 for students and children 5–18 years, free for under 5s, $27.50 for seniors; Beyond all Boundaries and Final Mission: additional $7

....

■ The museum has a dedicated parking garage located at 1024 Magazine Street.

■ There are two on-site restaurants: the retro-chic Jeri Nims Soda Shoppe and the slightly more formal American Sector restaurant, both serving sandwiches, wraps, salads, and grills.

5 U.S. Freedom Pavilion

Restored combat aircraft, tanks, and displays of the uniforms worn by all U.S. service branches occupy this huge gallery **(above)**. The "What Would You Do" interactive exhibit here poses visitors with sticky questions based on real wartime decisions.

6 The Battle of the Bulge

With a simulated snowy Ardennes forest setting, this exhibit explores the six-week Battle of the Bulge. Artifact cases and recorded oral histories take visitors through this pivotal engagement.

8 Road to Tokyo

A re-creation of the bridge of the aircraft carrier USS *Enterprise* serves as the setting for this exhibit. Displays here trace the Pacific War and the trail from Pearl Harbor to Tokyo from the American perspective.

9 The D-Day Invasion

The historic landings at Normandy on June 6, 1944 are recalled via a treasure trove of photos, recorded testimonials, bits of Nazi Germany's Atlantic Wall fortifications, and sand from the original landing beaches.

TOP 10 ★ The Historic New Orleans Collection

Founded in 1966, The Historic New Orleans Collection (THNOC) is a museum and research and publishing center combined into one, with its efforts toward telling the cultural and historical story of New Orleans and the greater Gulf South. The collection is spread across three sites that are themselves located within historical buildings. THNOC has no admission fee and regularly hosts lectures, musical events, readings, and other educational engagements.

2 Noreen B. Lapeyre Gallery

Displays of signage (left) from old streetcars and steamboats, including the Jim Crow signs that segregated public transport by race, showcase how the city has evolved.

3 French Quarter After Dark

This immersive film traces both the French Quarter's nightlife from the 1700s to the present day and "dark" events such as the 19th-century yellow fever epidemic.

1 The Entrance Touchscreen

As visitors enter the museum, they come across an interactive touchscreen map (below) of the French Quarter. This engaging exhibit introduces you to the area's many historical buildings, which can be visited on self-guided itineraries provided by the THNOC app.

4 Williams Research Center

THNOC's archives are housed in this research center. Its stately Reading Room contains some 30,000 library items and 500,000 prints, photographs, and paintings.

WILLIAMS RESIDENCE

THNOC's original campus at 533 Royal Street includes the former home of the institution's founders Lewis Kemper Williams and Leila Moore. When the couple renovated the property in 1938, at which time the French Quarter was at risk of demolition, they kick-started preservation efforts and patronage of the arts, which has defined New Orleans tourism since. Tours of the historical house are offered by THNOC.

7 The Garvey Gallery

Material exhibits **(left)**, as well as an interactive console in this gallery, detail the stories of the different cultures and groups that have made up New Orleans – from Indigenous peoples to immigrants from Haiti, Germany, China, and other nations.

9 Third-Floor Terrace at 520 Royal St

This terrace offers an overhead view of a typical 19th-century French Quarter courtyard. The space used to be more functional than decorative – old photos show this courtyard with hanging laundry lines and wandering chickens. The courtyard includes a glass-sealed display of an archaeological dig.

10 Portrait of a Free Woman of Color

Dating from 1837, this painting was incorrectly restored in 1988 to depict the sitter as a servant. THNOC has since corrected the painting to its original form in a step against the erasure of Black histories.

THNOC's grand portrait gallery

5 LeBlanc Gallery

This section includes architectural elements, sketches, and blueprints of some of the city's iconic buildings, along with old theater playbills, lobby cards, and posters on movies filmed in the French Quarter. There's also an original script page from local author Tennessee Williams' *A Streetcar Named Desire*.

6 LGBTQ+ Exhibits

A corner of the Garvey Gallery displays a flyer for a 1998 memorial for the men who died in the 1973 arson attack on UpStairs Lounge, a gay bar. There is also a poster from Gay Fest 1981, a party that was responsible for kick-starting the city's busy LGBTQ+ events calendar.

8 Fields Gallery

Playbills for local opera troupes, including an advertisement for the first performance ever held at the French Opera House, can be seen here. There is also a copy of a 1736 music booklet given to the Ursulines nuns, which is the only evidence of music in New Orleans in the 18th century.

> **NEED TO KNOW**
>
> **MAP M4**
>
> *Royal Street campuses:* 520 & 533 Royal St; 504-523-4662; open 9:30am–4:30pm Tue–Sat, 10:30am–4:30pm Sun; www.hnoc.org
>
> *Williams Research Center:* 410 Chartres St; 504-598-7171; open 9:30am–4:30pm Tue–Sat
>
> ■ The Shop at The Collection, located at 520 Royal Street, sells historical photos of local backstreet culture, books for adults and kids, jewelry, crafts, and clothes by local artists.
>
> ■ The on-site Café Cour has drinks, sandwiches, salads, and small and medium plates that draw on the region's culinary history.

🔟 ⭐ Mississippi Riverfront

New Orleans owes its very existence to the Mississippi River, an iconic feature on the country's cultural, historic, and economic landscape. Businesses, attractions, and special events make this area a must-see for any visitor to New Orleans. A great place for a stroll or a picnic, the walkway offers sweeping river views and is dotted with public art and departure points for cruises. The riverfront is within walking distance of the Warehouse District, the CBD, and many of the best hotels and restaurants.

1 Woldenberg Riverfront Park

This waterfront space (above) is one of the most pleasant spots in the downtown area. The park hosts events, concerts, and festivals throughout the year.

2 The Outlet Collection at Riverwalk

This vast indoor complex is two blocks long and faces the Mississippi River. Shop at a variety of retailers and enjoy some of the very best local delicacies that are on offer here.

3 Ernest N. Morial Convention Center

This is the largest convention-center space on a single level in the entire country. It hosts some of the biggest and most prestigious conventions in the world. The center also features state-of-the-art technology.

4 Creole Queen

One of the best ways to experience the Mississippi River is on a two-hour dinner cruise on the *Creole Queen* (left), a traditional paddlewheel steamboat.

GETTING AROUND THE RIVERFRONT

The riverfront is a vital part of the downtown area. Just across from the JAX Brewery, there is a ticketing kiosk where visitors can purchase tickets for river cruises (some including dinner). Transportation in and around the riverfront is frequent and convenient. The streetcar stops near the Aquarium and runs until 10:30pm daily, while the ferry from downtown to the West Bank of New Orleans runs until just after midnight.

JAX Brewery (5)

A working brewery from 1891 to the mid–1970s, today the riverside JAX building **(right)** houses shops, boutiques, and restaurants. A museum traces its history.

Public Art (7)

Striking sculptures such as John T. Scott's abstract *Ocean Song* and Franco Alessandrini's traditional *Monument to the Immigrant* dot the area along the riverfront.

Moonwalk (8)

Running the full length of the riverfront, the Moonwalk is a heavily traveled walkway. Along this stretch there are benches where you can relax and watch the river.

Crescent Park (10)

Sitting right on the edge of the river, this green space *(see p98)* is a part of the French Market District. It is a popular hangout for joggers, cyclists, and dog walkers. Music and other events are regularly hosted at pavilions here.

Spanish Plaza (6)

Located between the Audubon Aquarium of the Americas *(see p79)* and The Outlet Collection at Riverwalk, the Spanish Plaza is the site of year-round special events and concerts.

Riverfront Streetcar (9)

The bright-red Mississippi Riverfront streetcar **(right)** stops intermittently along the riverfront at all the major shopping and tourist attractions.

Around the Mississippi Riverfront

NEED TO KNOW

MAP N4–5

The Outlet Collection at Riverwalk: 500 Port of New Orleans; 504-522-1555; www.riverwalk neworleans.com

Ernest N. Morial Convention Center: 900 Convention Center Blvd; www.mccno.com

Creole Queen: 1 Poydras St; 504-529-4567; cruise timings vary, check website; adm $39–95 for adults, $10–40 for under 12s; www.creolequeen.com

JAX Brewery: 600 Decatur St; 504-566-7245; open 10am–7pm daily; www. jacksonbrewery.com

Crescent Park: 1008 N. Peters St.; www.crescent parknola.org

■ For refreshments head to The Outlet Collection at Riverwalk or to the French Market on nearby N. Peters Street *(p90)* where you can grab a nice lunch.

Following pages Crescent City Connection Bridge on the Mississippi River

TOP 10 ⭐ Jackson Square

The elegant centerpiece of the French Quarter, Jackson Square is a lively meeting place. Known as the Place d'Armes in the 1700s, it was later renamed for the Battle of New Orleans general, Andrew Jackson. His statue dominates the square, with the St. Louis Cathedral providing a majestic backdrop. Quaint shops line the edge of the park, and artists, palm readers, and musicians sell their wares and perform here daily.

1 The Presbytère

Dating to circa 1791, this building *(see p49)* is part of the Louisiana State Museum. It houses a fabulous Mardi Gras exhibit **(above)**, as well as some of the finest ball gowns and costumes from past Mardi Gras celebrations.

JACKSON SQUARE IN THE MOVIES

If Jackson Square looks familiar even on a first visit, it may be because it has been used as a backdrop in several movies. The square was a featured location in *The Curious Case of Benjamin Button* (2008). The New Orleans Office of Film and Video fields frequent requests for filming on the square, with starring roles in TV shows such as *CSI: New Orleans*, *Treme*, and *Memphis Beat*. Fans of Elvis Presley might recognize the backdrop from his film *King Creole*.

2 Street Musicians

New Orleans is best known for its food and music. The grassroots musicians **(below)**, who make their living playing on the streets, are most at home in the heart of Jackson Square.

3 St. Louis Cathedral

This is the oldest continuously active Catholic church in the country **(above)**, first built in 1727, and rebuilt twice since then. The dramatic lighting makes even the back of the church look imposing.

4 Andrew Jackson Statue

Commander of the American forces at the Battle of New Orleans and 7th president of the U.S., Andrew Jackson is commemorated with a bronze equestrian statue in the center of Jackson Square.

5 Place d'Armes Hotel

Conveniently located right on the edge of the square, the Place d'Armes Hotel is a charming place close to most of the attractions of the French Quarter. Restored 18th- and 19th-century buildings surround a courtyard.

Map of Jackson Square

8 Artists' Community

New Orleans artists do not all need a studio. Many of them work and sell their creations **(below)** in and around Jackson Square itself.

10 Pedestrian Walkway

Jackson Square's perimeter is lined with stores and boutiques. Pedestrians can spend hours strolling among the musicians, jesters, and artists who work here.

6 Pontalba Apartment Buildings

The oldest apartments in the country (built in the mid-1800s) are among some of the city's most enviable addresses.

9 Faulkner House Books

This two-story building was once home to author William Faulkner. Today, it is a National Historic Landmark and houses a fine bookstore.

7 The Cabildo

The site of the 1803 Louisiana Purchase (see p40) and one of the Louisiana State Museum's buildings, the Cabildo **(below)** features artifacts, artworks, and rotating exhibits highlighting local history.

NEED TO KNOW

MAP M5

The Presbytère and the Cabildo: Jackson Square; 504-568-6968; open 9am–4pm Tue–Sun; adm $10 for adults, $8 for children

St. Louis Cathedral: 615 Pere Antoine Alley; 504-525-9585; tours: timings vary, ask during your visit; www.stlouiscathedral.org

Place d'Armes Hotel: 625 St. Ann St; 504-524-4531; www.placedarmes.com; $$

Pontalba Apartment Buildings: St. Peter and St. Ann Sts

Faulkner House Books: 624 Pirate's Alley; 504-524-2940; www.faulknerhousebooks.com

▪ Take a slow stroll past the many artists who turn the square into a public gallery with their canvases and sculptures.

▪ Try the famous coffee and *beignets* at the Café du Monde (see p101).

🔟 ⭐ Royal Street

One of the oldest streets in the city, picturesque Royal Street features some of the country's best antiques stores and art galleries. Antiques collectors travel here from all over the world to shop at European-style boutiques and visit glass artists and purveyors of fine collectibles. Visitors can stay at historic hotels, enjoy leisurely breakfasts at sunny cafés, or indulge in gourmet cuisine at the numerous specialty restaurants.

1 The Cornstalk Hotel
Aptly named because of the cornstalk design on the iron fence around the building, this fine hotel (see p116) with antique furnishings has old-world charm.

2 Fleur de Paris
The only boutique of its kind in the South, this lovely shop features couture clothing as well as stunning hats for women, all designed and created at the store itself.

3 Court of Two Sisters
This historic restaurant **(below)** was originally a shop owned by two Creole sisters. Today, it is owned by two bro-thers, but it still retains its original name and is famous for its daily buffet accompanied by live Dixieland jazz.

4 Gallier House
Designed by James Gallier Jr., this grand 19th-century mansion is an amalgam of Creole and American styles. It also inspired local author Anne Rice (see p41) to create Louis and Lestat's home in her book *Interview with the Vampire*.

Map of Royal Street

5 Mr. B's Bistro
Located at the corner of Royal and Iberville streets, this restaurant's (see p61) chief draw is its Creole cuisine. Mr. B's signa-ture dish is the "Gumbo Ya-Ya" (gumbo with pork sausage and chicken).

Picturesque building on Royal Street

NEED TO KNOW

MAP L4

The Cornstalk Hotel: 915 Royal St; 504-523-1515; www.cornstalkhotel.com

Fleur de Paris: 523 Royal St; 504-525-1899

Court of Two Sisters: 613 Royal St; 504-522-7261; $$$

Gallier House: 1132 Royal St; 504-525-5661; call for timings; adm $15.45 for adults, $12.36 for children and seniors; www.hgghh.org

Mr. B's Bistro: 201 Royal St; 504-523-2078; $$$

Hotel Monteleone: 214 Royal St; 504-523-3341

Café Amelie: 912 Royal St; 504-412-8965; $$$

The Supreme Court of Louisiana: 400 Royal St; 504-310-2300

Omni Royal Orleans: 621 St. Louis St; 504-529-5333

Rodrigue Studio: 730 Royal St; 504-581-4244; open 11am–5pm Mon–Sat, noon–5pm Sun

■ Do not miss the array of interesting boutiques tucked away on the little side streets in the area.

The Supreme Court of Louisiana (8)

A massive face-lift has restored this huge stone and marble structure **(right)** to its former glory. The Beaux Arts-style building dates back to 1910 and represents the city's architectural heritage.

(6) Hotel Monteleone

Founded in 1886, this grand family-run hotel *(see p116)* is a New Orleans landmark. A favorite haunt of 20th-century writers, it is still popular with current literati, including Anne Rice and John Grisham.

(9) Omni Royal Orleans

Considered one of the area's premier properties, this hotel *(see p117)* was built on the site of the 1836 St. Louis Hotel. It has a rooftop pool, and houses the Rib Room, one of the finest restaurants in the city.

(7) Café Amelie

Enjoy superb Louisiana fare – including shrimp and grits – at this café *(see p58)* where diners can bask in the sun. The Princess of Monaco courtyard is 150 years old.

(10) Rodrigue Studio

The renowned "Blue Dog" paintings **(left)** were created here by Louisiana artist George Rodrigue. Today, his typically Southern art is highly valued.

UPSCALE DINING ON ROYAL STREET

It is only fitting that some of the best spots for fine-dining in the city are on this magnificent French Quarter street. A good day on Royal Street would include breakfast at Café Amelie, lunch at the Rib Room, and dinner at Mr. B's Bistro. In between, plan a leisurely cocktail hour at the stylish bar at Omni Royal Orleans Hotel.

Shopping for Antiques

Walking sticks at The Brass Monkey

1 The Brass Monkey

This store *(see p93)* has the largest collection of Limoges boxes in town. The inventory also includes antique walking sticks, Venetian glass, and medical instruments.

2 Royal Antiques Ltd.

Housing some of the most elegant pieces in the French Quarter, this store's *(see p93)* collection includes lovely French mirrors, Biedermeier furniture, and Chippendale chairs.

3 Maison Royale

MAP M4 ▪ 501 Royal St ▪ 504-524-5045
Located right in the heart of the French Quarter, Maison Royale features vintage jewelry and beautiful antique works of art.

4 Moss Antiques

This store *(see p93)* is a specialist in silver, period jewelry, chandeliers, antique furnishings, and Limoges enamel. The art and sculpture is also noteworthy.

5 Harris Antiques Ltd.

MAP M3 ▪ 233 Royal St ▪ 504-523-1605

Harris has one of the largest selections of 18th-, 19th-, and early 20th-century French, Italian, and English furniture, grandfather clocks, and French mantle clocks, as well as antique bronzes and marble sculptures.

6 Keil's Antiques

MAP M4 ▪ 325 Royal St ▪ 504-522-4552

This three-story shop offers thousands of French and English antiques, including chandeliers, jewelry, furniture, and tabletop items. The proprietors of Keil's also own Moss Antiques and Royal Antiques on the same street. The best thing about this store is that there is something for every budget.

7 M.S. Rau Antiques

MAP M4 ▪ 630 Royal St ▪ 888-557-2406

This store has been around since 1912. It is stocked with beautiful jewelry, 18th- and 19th- century fine art, and *objets d'art*. M.S. Rau is also famous for its impressive range of American and European antique furniture.

Gramophone at M.S. Rau Antiques

8 Ida Manheim Antiques

MAP M4 ▪ 409 Royal St ▪ 504-620-4114

Originally a small cabinet shop, today this family-owned store has a fine selection of European and Asian furnishings, porcelains, jade, silver, and paintings.

⑨ James H. Cohen & Sons, Inc.
MAP M4 ▪ 437 Royal St
▪ 504-522-3305

This is the only shop in New Orleans that specializes in rare coins, antique firearms, swords, and unusual collectibles such as old ballot boxes and World War I telescopes.

⑩ French Antique Shop
MAP M3 ▪ 225 Royal St
▪ 504-524-9861

This family-owned store offers a great collection of antique chandeliers and lamps, plus fine art, furniture, and tapestries. Located in the second block of Royal Street, this is the perfect place to begin shopping.

ART SHOPPING ON ROYAL STREET

The art scene in New Orleans is a vibrant and integral part of the city's culture and economy. Galleries flourish in virtually every nook of the city, showcasing works by artists ranging from fresh local talent to renowned names. Exciting new trends and styles have developed out of the city's eclectic culture, and New Orleans is considered to be a key hub of art in the U.S. Serious collectors travel across the world to catch the latest showings. On the first Saturday night of each month, galleries throughout the city hold a wine and cheese open house, where they welcome all visitors to view their latest collections.

Boutique art galleries give visitors a glimpse of the city's eclectic art scene.

TOP 10
UNIQUE GALLERIES ON ROYAL STREET

1 Rodrigue Studio (Home of the "Blue Dog")

2 Gallery Burguieres

3 Caliche & Pao Gallery

4 Angela King Gallery

5 Graphite Galleries LLC

6 Fischer-Gambino

7 Gallery Rinard

8 Elliott Gallery LLC

9 Gallery for Fine Photography

10 Martin Lawrence Gallery

TOP 10 ⭐ Bourbon Street

This iconic French Quarter street never sleeps. It dates back to 1718, when it was known as Rue Bourbon, and still retains some of the original 18th-century architecture, which can be seen on a leisurely walk down the street. With around-the-clock live music, parties, and all-night bars and clubs, Bourbon Street has an atmosphere of revelry that is unmatched in the city. Renowned restaurants lie interspersed between unique shops and vendors. A night out on Bourbon Street is a once-in-a-lifetime experience.

1 Pat O'Brien's
The infamous "Hurricane" cocktail was invented here in the 1940s. Today, this bar **(below)** offers a lively ambience.

2 Famous Door
This raucous club is packed every night. The Famous Door is a typical all-night Bourbon Street nightclub.

3 LGBTQ+ Entertainment
Many restaurants and bars here cater to the city's LGBTQ+ community. Anchoring the district is the lively Bourbon Pub Parade.

4 Cat's Meow Karaoke Club
With one of the most in-demand stages in the French Quarter, Cat's Meow has pulsating karaoke music, which permeates right through the whole block.

Neon-lit clubs and bars on Bourbon Street

NEED TO KNOW

MAP M3

Pat O'Brien's Bar: 718 St. Peter St; 504-525-4823

Famous Door: 339 Bourbon St; 504-598-4334

Bourbon Pub Parade: 801 Bourbon St; 504-529-2107

Cat's Meow Karaoke Club: 701 Bourbon St; 504-523-2788; www.cats karaoke.com

Royal Sonesta Hotel: 300 Bourbon St; 504-586-0300; www.royalsonesta.com

Clover Grill: 900 Bourbon St; 504-598-1010

Preservation Hall: 726 St. Peter St; 504-522-2841

Bourbon House Restaurant: 144 Bourbon St; 504-522-0111; $$$

Lafitte's Blacksmith Shop Bar: 941 Bourbon St; 504-593-9761

Galatoire's Restaurant: 209 Bourbon St; 504-525-2021; closed Mon; $$$

■ It is legal to carry alcohol on Bourbon Street. All the bars have "to go" cups.

For a key to restaurant price ranges see p77

**Map of
Bourbon
Street**

7 Preservation Hall

New Orleans jazz echoes through this legendary music hall **(above)**. Veteran jazz musicians and new acts still play here every week.

8 Bourbon House Restaurant

Old New Orleans charm blends seamlessly with a contemporary vibe in this Creole restaurant *(see p95)*, in the first block of Bourbon Street. Ask for the Bourbon House Restaurant frozen-bourbon milk punch.

LIVING ON BOURBON STREET

Although known for its unique nightlife, Bourbon Street is also home for many New Orleanians. Many of the facades of the street-facing houses are actually the backs of the homes, built to face lush interior courtyards. Every October, the Historic Bourbon Street Foundation sponsors a "Treasures of Bourbon Street" tour, featuring centuries-old Creole townhouses, cottages, and period architecture.

5 Royal Sonesta Hotel

The Royal Sonesta *(see p117)* occupies a busy corner of Bourbon Street. Enjoy delicious oysters at The Desire Bar, and watch live performances at The Jazz Playhouse.

6 Clover Grill

This late-night joint is a favorite when it comes to needing something filling and delicious at all hours of the day or night. Enjoy burgers grilled on a hubcap and served in a 1950s retro setting.

9 Lafitte's Blacksmith Shop Bar

This late-18th-century Creole cottage **(below)** may look decrepit, but it houses one of the French Quarter's nicest watering holes. This is one of the best spots for people-watching in the area.

10 Galatoire's Restaurant

A wonderful place to dine in the city, Galatoire's has an old-world feel and fabulous cuisine. The soufflé potatoes are a must-try.

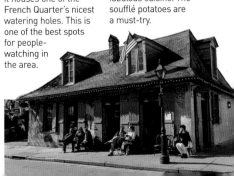

TOP 10 ★ Mardi Gras

New Orleans bills its annual Mardi Gras celebration as "the biggest street party in the world." More than a million visitors gather in the city up to three weeks before the festival. Lavish parades are staged by various clubs, or "krewes," along with street gatherings and parties. New Orleans is the place to be during this time to let your hair down, don an outrageous costume, vie for beads thrown from parade floats, and generally party hard for the last time before Lent.

1 Bourbon Street Awards Costume Contest

This LGBTQ+ costume contest, held on Mardi Gras afternoon, showcases some of the most striking and imaginative costumes of the festival. Staged on Bourbon Street, it attracts thousands of locals and visitors alike.

2 Krewe of Rex Parade

The crown jewel of New Orleans' Mardi Gras is the Krewe of Rex Parade (right). Rex has reigned as King of the Carnival since he first appeared in 1872, and he has since defined the festival with the royal colors of purple, green, and gold.

3 Krewe of Zulu Parade

Just before the Rex Parade is the Krewe of Zulu (above) on the morning of Mardi Gras. The Zulu Social Aid and Pleasure Club produces one of the most festive parades, inspired by the renowned warriors of the southern African nation.

4 Krewe of Endymion Parade

Considered one of the longest and most elaborate parades, Endymion rolls out on the Saturday before Mardi Gras. The Endymion ball is one of the most popular in town and continues all night.

5 Krewe of Armenius Gay Mardi Gras Ball

The LGBTQ+ community produces some of the most elaborate Mardi Gras balls. The Krewe of Armenius throws camp and uproariously funny balls. Their costumes are among the best in the city.

BLAINE KERN'S MARDI GRAS WORLD

Blaine Kern is the master Mardi Gras float designer and builder in New Orleans, and his Mardi Gras World is a year-round facility open to the public. Here, visitors can see how the props and floats are conceived, designed, and constructed. Giant character heads and extravagant floats from past Mardi Gras festivals are displayed in this building. The space is also rented out for private parties and receptions (see p48).

Krewe of Bacchus (6)

The Bacchus Parade **(right)** on the Sunday before Mardi Gras features more than 25 floats, including some of the largest and longest, such as the King Kong, the Queen Kong, and the heralded Bachagator.

(10) Mardi Gras Parades on St. Charles Avenue

On Mardi Gras, groups of friends and families stake out their territory along the historic St. Charles Avenue to watch the Rex and Zulu parades, as well as the "everyman" truck parades that follow them.

(7) Krewe du Vieux

If it can be mocked, the Krewe du Vieux will do so in their highly anticipated parade. Typical themes of this popular group tend to be satirical and bawdy.

(8) Krewe of Muses

Named for the daughters of Zeus in ancient Greek mythology, Muses is one of the few all-female krewes. They delight crowds by throwing lavishly decorated shoes on their parade route from Magazine and Jefferson.

(9) Krewe of Barkus Dog Parade

Every year, dog owners dress themselves and their pets in matching costumes and parade through the French Quarter **(left)**. Dog parade themes include "A Street-Bark Named Desire" as well as "Tail House Rock."

NEED TO KNOW

■ Mardi Gras is celebrated on the Tuesday before Lent, but celebrations begin as early as January 6, with the night of the Epiphany (the festival marking the revelation of God as Jesus Christ).

■ The crowd is usually well behaved, but be careful with your personal items. Stay on streets that are highly populated. Be warned that a lot of alcohol is consumed during Mardi Gras, so try to steer clear of drunken revelers.

■ Bars are open citywide during Mardi Gras, although not necessarily for food. Either bring your own or try the snacks available from street vendors. On St. Charles Avenue, people generally bring their own coolers and snacks with them.

Canal Street

One of the broadest streets in the U.S., the 170-ft (52-m) wide Canal Street runs across New Orleans, from the Mississippi to Lake Pontchartrain. The main activity is around the CBD, where luxury hotels, upscale restaurants, and fine retail establishments line both sides of the street. The Canal streetcar line runs down the middle of the thoroughfare, providing access to Mid-City and the theaters.

2 Canal Place
Located right by the Mississippi, this complex of offices, stores, restaurants, and theaters **(left)** is dominated by the upscale Saks Fifth Avenue.

3 Joy Theater
Built in 1947 as a movie palace, the Art Deco Joy Theater was transformed into a live performance space in 2011. This state-of-the-art venue now hosts live music, stand-up comedy, and theatrical performances.

4 Palace Café
Housed in an elegant early-20th-century building, the three-story Palace Café *(see p85)* serves contemporary, delicious Creole cuisine. Do not miss the crabmeat cheesecake and the white chocolate bread pudding.

Streetcars on Canal Street

CANAL STREETCAR

To take in the city's sights at a leisurely pace, the Canal streetcar is a great option. This is the best way to see the architecture and layout of the city, all the way from the Mississippi to the historic cemeteries in the Mid-City area, while the Rampart-St. Claude line serves the artsy Faubourg Marigny and Bywater neighborhoods. Tickets cost $1.25.

1 The Ritz-Carlton, New Orleans
A historic structure that once housed a department store, this building has been elegantly refashioned into the Ritz-Carlton Hotel *(see p116)*. The hotel has 450 guest rooms and is home to a world-class spa, stylish restaurant M Bistro, and nightly live jazz.

6 Harrah's New Orleans Casino
This casino is the only land-based one in the city (the other two are on boats). The property includes table games, slot machines, fine restaurants, a luxurious hotel, and an ice bar.

5 Canal Street Ferry Line
Commuters traveling from the East Bank of New Orleans to the West Bank often use the ferry line at the foot of Canal Street. Passengers can also drive their cars onto the ferry **(below)**.

8 Audubon Aquarium of the Americas

Explore the underwater worlds of nearly 500 species of aquatic animals, including jellyfish, rare seahorses, and playful otters, among others, at this vast aquarium **(left)**.

10 Rubensteins

The city's oldest house of fine fashion, Rubensteins stands at the corner of Canal Street and St. Charles Avenue. This menswear store has been providing quality fabrics and tailoring since 1924.

7 Saenger Theatre

Originally a cinema, this restored historic landmark theater *(see p81)* resembles a Renaissance Italian courtyard, replete with classical arches and columns that frame the stage. Touring Broadway shows, comedians, and musicians feature here.

9 The Roosevelt New Orleans

This grand hotel *(see p116)* opened in 1893 as the Grunewald, and is now part of the Waldorf Astoria hotel group. It features the historic Sazerac Bar and the legendary Blue Room, used for weddings and private events.

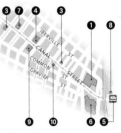

Map of Canal Street

NEED TO KNOW

MAP E4

The Ritz-Carlton, New Orleans: 921 Canal St; 504-524-1331

Canal Place: 333 Canal St; 504-522-9200

Joy Theater: 1200 Canal St; 504-528-9569; www.the joytheater.com

Canal Street Ferry Line: 1 Canal St; ferry to Algiers Point every 15 minutes; www.norta.com

Harrah's New Orleans Casino: 8 Canal St; 504-533-6000; www. harrahsneworleans.com

Saenger Theatre: 1111 Canal St; 504-525-1052; www.saengernola.com

Audubon Aquarium of the Americas: 1 Canal St; 504-861-2537; www.audubon natureinstitute.org

The Roosevelt New Orleans: 130 Roosevelt Way; 504-648-1200

Rubensteins: 102 St. Charles Ave; 504-581-6666

■ Cross Canal Street at designated cross walks only.

The Top 10 of Everything

**The jazz band at New Orleans'
historic Preservation Hall**

🔟 Moments in History

Jean Baptiste Le Moyne de Bienville

① Founding of New Orleans (1718)

Jean Baptiste Le Moyne de Bienville of the French Mississippi Company founded a colony on the Lower Mississippi and named it "La Nouvelle Orléans." Surrounded by the river, lakes, and swamps, it also became known as the Île d'Orléans. The first ships carrying enslaved workers from Africa arrived a year later. Such was the demand for free slave labor, that the number of enslaved Africans soon outnumbered white colonists.

② New Orleans becomes a Spanish Colony (1763)

The city was ceded to the Spanish in 1763 by Louis XV. However, the French settlers rebelled and forced governor Antonio de Ulloa to abdicate. It was General Alexander O'Reilly who established Spanish control in 1768. Thereafter, the Spanish encouraged trade and turned the city into a commercial hub.

③ The Great French Quarter Fire (1788)

Of the 100 buildings in New Orleans, 856 were destroyed by a fire on Good Friday in 1788. At the time, the city had only two fire vehicles, and both were destroyed. After the fire, the city was rebuilt with Spanish-style colonial architecture.

④ The Civil War (1861–65)

At the outbreak of the Civil War, New Orleans was the largest city in the Southern Confederacy (and the sixth-largest in the U.S.). The city was quickly captured by the Union navy in 1862, setting the stage for an occupation characterized by martial law, civil disobedience, and the eventual emancipation of the city's enslaved population.

⑤ Reconstruction (1865–77)

Even as liberated African Americans founded schools and were elected to political office, they were subjected to massacres by white supremacists. By 1877, former Confederates and their sympathizers took control of the state, suppressed the Black vote, enforced public segregation, and raised monuments to Southern generals to proclaim the return of the old order.

⑥ World Cotton Exposition (1884)

The 1884 World Cotton Exposition lasted six months. Up to a third of all cotton produced in the U.S. was handled in New Orleans, home of the Cotton Exchange. However, despite its scale, this fair was a financial disaster riddled with debt and corruption, especially as treasurer Edward A. Burke absconded with much of its budget.

Illustration of World Cotton Exposition

7 Desegregation (1954)

The era spanning the 1950s and 60s was marked by social change as the Civil Rights Movement gained ground. In its landmark 1954 ruling Brown v. Board of Education, the U.S. Supreme Court finally outlawed racial segregation in public schools.

Brown v. Board of Education lawyers

8 Louisiana World Exposition (1984)

The centerpiece of this event was a gondola lift that ferried millions of visitors across the Mississippi River. The fair was the precursor to a major redevelopment of the riverfront area.

9 Hurricane Katrina (2005)

The largest natural disaster in the U.S., Hurricane Katrina hit New Orleans on August 29, 2005. The failure of the levees caused massive flooding and destruction. Thousands were displaced (disproportionately, but not exclusively African American), causing major re-ordering of city demographics.

10 Removal of Confederate Monuments (2017)

In 2017, the City Council removed many controversial Confederate monuments despite fierce protest, and declared them a public nuisance. Among them was a statue of General Robert E. Lee, commander of the Confederate armies. Three more statues commemorating Confederate generals and the Crescent City White League were also removed.

TOP 10 NEW ORLEANS FIGURES

1 Marie Laveau (1801–81)
Known as New Orleans' "Voodoo Queen," Laveau practiced the religion that originated in West Africa.

2 Louis Armstrong (1901–71)
Armstrong, also known as "Satchmo," is globally remembered as a premier jazz trumpeter and singer.

3 Mahalia Jackson (1911–72)
Long heralded as the "Queen of Gospel Music," Jackson recorded 35 albums during her career.

4 Tennessee Williams (1911–83)
Playwright Williams captured the angst of the American South in his works, including *The Glass Menagerie*.

5 Truman Capote (1924–84)
During his controversial career, Capote authored some of the best-selling novels of his time, including *In Cold Blood*.

6 Anne Rice (b.1941)
A master scribe of horror novels, Rice is the author of the popular *Vampire Chronicles* series.

7 Ellen Degeneres (b.1958)
The famous comedienne hosts a well-known talk show, and has appeared on stage and in movies.

8 Emeril Lagasse (b.1959)
Now a TV personality, Lagasse is renowned as a chef, restaurateur, and cookbook author.

9 Harry Connick, Jr. (b.1967)
This award-winning jazz musician is also a talk show host and movie star.

10 Jon Batiste (b.1986)
A multi-instrumentalist, bandleader, TV personality, and winner of many Grammy awards, including Best Album for *We Are*.

Jon Batiste at the Grammy awards in 2022

🔟 **Architectural Highlights**

The beautiful, elaborately decorated interior of St. Patrick's Church

1 St. Patrick's Church

The subtle Gothic exterior of the church (see p82) belies its ornate interior. Built in the early 19th century, the original building was overhauled to create a much grander structure with a 185-ft- (56-m-) high bell tower. The altar, windows, and doorways are in Gothic style, while 16 stunning stained-glass windows form a beautiful half dome over the altar.

2 Lafitte's Blacksmith Shop Bar

The oldest building in the French Quarter was built in 1772 by alleged slave-traders Pierre and Jean Lafitte. Considered to be the longest continually operating bar room (see p32) in the country, it is still lit by candlelight.

3 The Supreme Court of Louisiana

The Supreme Court of Louisiana building (see p29) is an imposing edifice made of stone and marble. The 1910 structure is an example of Beaux-Arts architecture, with its arched windows and Classical pilasters. Once in ruins, this landmark building was restored to its previous glory with a major $50-million renovation.

4 Hotel Monteleone

The 1886 luxury hotel (see p116) underwent a $60-million renovation in 2004, but has retained its original grandeur. Grab a cocktail at the revolving Carousel Bar.

5 Caesars Superdome

This stadium (see p80) is home to the New Orleans Saints American football team. The dome covers the world's largest steel-constructed space unob- structed by posts. Considered to be one of the premier sports venues in the country, the stadium will host the National Football League Super Bowl in 2025.

Caesars Superdome at night

6 The Cabildo

One of five properties making up the Louisiana State Museum, the Cabildo (see p27) was originally built in 1788, destroyed in the fire of 1795, and rebuilt. The Cabildo was the site where the Louisiana Purchase (see p40) was signed in 1803.

7 Napoleon House

Now a restaurant (see p95), this early 19th-century landmark was originally the home of New Orleans mayor, Nicholas Girod, who offered it as a refuge for Napoleon during the latter's imprisonment at St. Helena.

8 Pontalba Apartment Buildings

Built in 1849 by the French Baroness Pontalba, these apartment buildings (see p27), the oldest in the U.S., reflect both French and American architecture, with cast-iron galleries and Creole-style floor plans.

Pontalba Apartment Buildings

9 The Peristyle at City Park

MAP H2 ▪ 1 Palm Drive ▪ 504-482-4888 ▪ www.neworleanscitypark.com

The Neo-Classical Peristyle, built in 1907, is supported by massive Ionic columns and guarded by four stone lions. A stairway leads down to the picturesque Bayou Metairie waterway.

10 St. Louis Cathedral

The triple steeples of this Jackson Square landmark (see p90) make it one of the city's most striking and recognizable buildings. Inside, visitors can admire stained-glass windows, paintings, and a Rococo-style gilded altar.

TOP 10 PUBLIC ART SITES

A float at Mardi Gras World

1 Blaine Kern's Mardi Gras World
Watch carnival floats and figures being made at this warehouse (see p48).

2 Sydney and Walda Besthoff Sculpture Garden
The sculpture garden is an outdoor installation at NOMA (see pp12–15).

3 Enrique Alferez Sculptures
These graceful sculptures are artfully placed throughout the New Orleans City Park (see pp16–17).

4 Train Garden at Botanical Garden
This exhibit (see p17) features an eye-level New Orleans cityscape and running miniature train.

5 "Ocean Song" Kinetic Sculpture
MAP N5 ▪ Woldenberg Park
These eight pyramids depict the movement of the Mississippi.

6 Louis Armstrong Statue
The jazz legend is immortalized in this 12-ft- (4-m-) high statue (see p97) in Louis Armstrong Park.

7 Poydras Corridor
MAP N1 ▪ Poydras St
This rotating sculpture exhibition has included works by Southern artists of local and international acclaim.

8 Joan of Arc Maid of Orleans Statue
MAP L5 ▪ St. Philip St at Decatur St
This golden bronze statue is a replica of a 19th-century sculpture by French sculptor Emmanuel Frémiet.

9 Murals at Sazerac Bar
The Art Deco murals (see p116) in the Roosevelt hotel bar date to the 1930s.

10 Auseklis Ozols Murals at Windsor Court Hotel
These remarkable murals (see p116) depict famous New Orleanians in the Grill Room of the hotel.

🔟 Museums and Galleries

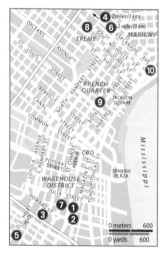

opened in 2000, the 56th anniversary of the Normandy invasion. It honors the Americans who took part in World War II. The museum also celebrates the New Orleans shipbuilder Andrew Higgins and explores the war's amphibious troop invasions.

③ Museum of the Southern Jewish Experience

MAP Q2 ▪ 818 Howard Ave ▪ 504-384-2480 ▪ Open 10am–5pm Wed–Mon ▪ Adm ▪ www.msje.org

The Jewish experience in the American South is explored in great detail at this small museum. It chronicles the discrimination, assimilation, and activism of the Jewish people through World War II, the Holocaust, and the Civil Rights Movement.

④ New Orleans Museum of Art

Established in 1911, the New Orleans Museum of Art, or NOMA (see pp12–15), is the oldest repository for art in the city. Permanent collections include rare French and American works, such as Claude Lorrain's *Ideal View of Tivoli*, and a stunning collection of art by Indigenous communities. Works by the masters, including Picasso, Renoir, Monet, Gauguin, and Pollock, are on display. The museum also includes a sculpture garden.

① Contemporary Arts Center New Orleans

Set in a stunning 30,000-sq-ft (2,800-sq-m) building, the Contemporary Arts Center (CAC) honors an eclectic collection of art genres covering music and dance, kinetic sculpture, drawings, and paintings. The CAC (see p80) also hosts multidisciplinary workshops in the performing arts.

② The National World War II Museum

Established by historian Stephen Ambrose, this museum (see pp18–19)

The exterior of The National World War II Museum

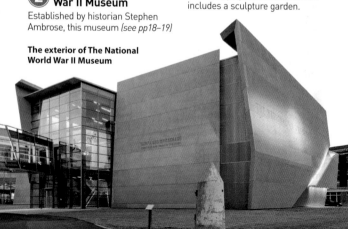

Southern Food & Beverage Museum

5 Southern Food & Beverage Museum

New Orleans locals joke that they are either eating, or talking about their next meal. So it's only fitting that there should be a museum dedicated to the city's vibrant culinary scene. The Southern Food & Beverage Museum – known locally as SoFAB – traces the history of food across all cultures, while the Museum of the American Cocktail, located in SoFAB, celebrates local drinks from absinthe to the Sazerac (see p57). The on-site restaurant (see p82) serves some Southern classics.

6 Louisiana Children's Museum

An air-conditioned retreat in summer, this museum (see p16) offers kids a hands-on experience, with indoor galleries, a wetlands area, and sensory gardens. It has outreach programs that make classroom teaching more vibrant.

7 Ogden Museum of Southern Art

The huge collection of contemporary art here (see p80) focuses on artists from the South. It includes pieces by father and son Benny and George Andrews, and works by folk artist Clementine Hunter. There is an after-hours program on Thursdays with live music and special exhibits.

8 New Orleans African American Museum

MAP K3 ▪ 1418 Governor Nicholls St ▪ 504-566-1136 ▪ Open 11am–4pm Wed–Sat ▪ Adm ▪ www.noaam.org

Located in Treme, home to the oldest African-American community in the country, this museum is housed in a Creole villa dating from 1828. Rotating exhibits chart the art, history, and culture of African Americans in New Orleans and the diaspora. Highlights include original African beads, masks, musical instruments, and religious objects from Congo.

9 The Historic New Orleans Collection

Set up in 1966, The Historic New Orleans Collection (see pp20–21) is a fascinating repository of manuscripts, artistic exhibits, and documents showcasing the varied cultures that have shaped the city. Used mainly as a resource by serious researchers, The Historic New Orleans Collection also attracts curious visitors who can learn about the city through its many historical artifacts.

The Historic New Orleans Collection

10 New Orleans Jazz Museum

Part of the Louisiana State Museum portfolio (see p92), the comprehensive New Orleans Jazz Museum's displays include a 1917 disc of the first jazz recording. The New Orleans Jazz Museum sits within the Old U.S. Mint, where visitors can also enjoy the collection of coins on display.

🔟 Off the Beaten Path

Lafitte Greenway, an urban retreat

1 Lafitte Greenway
MAP G3 ■ www.lafitte
greenway.org

A 3-mile- (5-km-) long linear park, Lafitte Greenway is beloved by New Orleans citizens looking to do some cycling, jogging, or exercise on the outdoor gym equipment scattered throughout the park. There are also permanent art installations along the way, as well as easy access to neighborhoods like Treme and Mid-City.

2 New Orleans Ghost Tour
MAP K4 ■ 718 N. Rampart St ■ 504-666-8300 ■ www.french quarterphantoms.com

The city's colorful and sometimes gory history means that downtown is as haunted a neighborhood as you'll find anywhere in the country. Three hundred years' worth of ghosts and ghouls inhabit the historic buildings of the French Quarter, and French Quarter Phantoms ghost tours bring the undead to life.

3 Cemetery Tours
Metairie Cemetery ■ 5100 Pontchartrain Blvd ■ Open 8am–5pm daily

Historically, people in New Orleans were buried in above-ground tombs rather than below. The popular myth is that this has to do with the city being below sea level, although it's actually a cultural choice. Some striking cemeteries can be found citywide; Metairie Cemetery is particularly well kept.

4 New Orleans Historic Voodoo Museum
MAP L4 ■ 724 Dumaine St ■ 504-680-0128

There are a lot of misconceptions about the practice of voodoo, and the New Orleans Historic Voodoo Museum is the best place to learn more about it. As well as exhibits on the history of voodoo and presentations of voodoo art, there is a voodoo priest on site to give readings and answer questions.

New Orleans Historic Voodoo Museum

5 Second Line Parades
www.wwoz.org/programs/inthestreet

Year-round, historic social clubs and benevolent associations organize big Second Line parades led by a brass band (the main/first line). People in festive dress follow the band, singing, dancing, and waving handkerchiefs. Visitors can join in or apply to the City for a permit to form their own line.

6 NOLA Social Ride
877-734-8687 ■ www.nola
socialride.org

Biking around New Orleans is always fun, but it's even better doing it with an enthusiastic bunch of locals who love to share their insider tips and knowledge of the city. This free ride-along takes place every week, with varying routes, a happy, friendly crowd, and the odd bar stop.

7 Museum of Death
MAP M3 ■ 227 Dauphine St
■ 504-593-3968 ■ www.museum
ofdeath.net/nola

The city has a unique perspective on death, and even funerals are celebratory affairs with music, dance, and a parade. What better location, then, for this strangely life-affirming museum dedicated to all things deathly, from rituals to serial killers to all manner of morbid artifacts.

8 Burlesque
Don't fall for the lurid strip clubs on Bourbon Street – there's a much more tasteful, artistic, and often tongue-in-cheek striptease option, supplied by New Orleans' thriving burlesque scene. Look at the calendars for the AllWays Lounge and Theatre (see p51) and the Hi-Ho Lounge (see p100). SoBou restaurant (see p59) has a delightfully kitsch "legs and eggs" burlesque brunch.

The New Orleans Pharmacy Museum

9 New Orleans Pharmacy Museum
The country's largest museum of pharmaceutical memorabilia, the New Orleans Pharmacy Museum (see p92) holds medical instruments, medicine vials, and prescriptions from the Civil War. It houses voodoo potions and a fascinating exhibit about epidemics of the 19th and 20th centuries, plus displays of the living quarters and architecture, with seasonal and special exhibits. Other than this, the museum provides educational programs.

10 New Orleans Cocktail Tours
MAP F3 ■ 400 Toulouse St
■ 504-569-1401 ■ www.
graylineneworleans.com

New Orleans is where some of the most famous cocktails in the world were created, such as the French 75 and the potent Sazerac (see p57). Visitors can have a fun history lesson as these tours stop at some of the most revered bars in the city. Note that only those aged 21 and over are eligible for this tour.

🔟 Children's Attractions

3 Jean Lafitte Swamp Tours

6601 Leo Kerner Lafitte Parkway, Marrero ■ 504-689-4186 ■ **Call ahead for adm details** ■ www.jeanlafitte swamptour.com

New Orleans is surrounded by swamps that are home to varied plants and wildlife. The best way to see this unique ecosystem is from a swamp boat. The tour is an exciting excursion for families.

4 Storyland

Children can enjoy a bit of old-fashioned fun at City Park's theme playground, Storyland *(see p17)*, where fairy tales are brought to life. These delightful creations include Captain Hook's pirate ship, Pinocchio's whale, and Jack and Jill's hill. Children can clamber all over the structures.

1 Crescent Park

Once an industrial wasteland, Crescent Park *(see p98)* was developed as part of the post-Hurricane Katrina revitalization project in 2015. It has wide open spaces for children to run and play as well as bike paths, dog runs, and superb views of the Mississippi. Just outside the park is Pizza Delicious *(see p101)*, which does takeouts – ideal for a picnic.

2 Audubon Zoo

This zoo *(see p73)* is home to a rare white tiger, orangutans, bears, and elephants, among others. Ride the Swamp Train, or fly through the trees on Kamba Kourse, an adventure ropes course, which towers above the giraffes. Kids will love the tree house and the slide on Monkey Hill. Viewing the animals in their simulated natural habitats is an entertaining and educational experience.

Zebras at Audubon Zoo

A character at Storyland

5 Blaine Kern's Mardi Gras World

MAP S5 ■ **1380 Port of New Orleans Place** ■ 504-361-7821 ■ **Open 9:30am–4:30pm daily** ■ **Adm** ■ www.mardi-grasworld.com

This vast warehouse displays Mardi Gras memorabilia, including floats and costumes. Most of the exhibits are created by the artist Blaine Kern.

The *Creole Queen* docked at the New Orleans port

6 Creole Queen

Nothing can give you the true feeling of being in New Orleans as much as a pleasant journey down the Mississippi River on the *Creole Queen (see p22)*, a paddlewheel steamboat. During the cruise, you will enjoy the captain's narration, rich with history and anecdotes, and see the city from the water. Visitors can also enjoy a dinner buffet and jazz music on the special Creole Queen dinner cruise.

7 Louisiana Children's Museum

Although it is an educational venue for children, this indoor-outdoor museum *(see p16)* will also appeal to inquisitive and playful adults. Captivating interactive displays, role-playing games, outdoor areas with sensory gardens and wetlands that encourage exploration, and a "floating classroom" make this a novel way to learn.

8 New Orleans City Park

The enormous New Orleans City Park *(see pp16–17)* dwarfs many of the U.S.'s other iconic urban green spaces such as New York's Central Park. With its playgrounds, acres of forest, and miles of trails (plus an outpost of Café du Monde that serves delicious French doughnuts), there is plenty to keep kids entertained here.

9 Audubon Aquarium of the Americas

At the edge of the Mississippi River, the aquarium *(see p79)* houses approximately 15,000 aquatic creatures and nearly 500 species. Do not miss the Great Maya Reef Tunnel, which allows a view of underwater life usually reserved for divers, and the Seahorse Gallery.

10 The Presbytère

First known as the Casa Curial (Ecclesiastical House), The Presbytère *(see pp26–7)* was built in 1813, sited on the former residence or "presbytery" of Capuchin monks, from which it gets its French name. It features exhibits on the impact of Hurricane Katrina and the city's recovery from it, plus a Mardi Gras section that has floats you can climb on, costumes, parade throws, and other carnival-time goodies that are a treat for all age groups.

Mardi Gras exhibits at The Presbytère

TOP10 **Performing Arts Venues**

1 BB's Stage Door Canteen

MAP Q3 ■ 945 Magazine St ■ 504-528-1943 ■ www.nationalww2museum.org

Performances at this venue in The National World War II Museum *(see p79)* include big bands, swing dancing, comedy, and jazz nights.

BB's Stage Door Canteen

2 Joy Theater

The Art Deco fixtures, including a glowing marquee sign, make this theater *(see pp36–7)* an evocative venue for comedy shows and other productions.

3 Saenger Theatre

More than $50 million was spent restoring the Saenger Theatre *(see p37)* to its former glory, complete with its famous blue domed ceilings and twinkling lights resembling the constellations of the night sky. It plays host to large musical acts, as well as the most popular touring Broadway and musical productions.

4 Lupin Theater, Tulane University

MAP B5 ■ 150 Dixon Hall Annexe, Tulane University ■ 504-865-5105 ■ www.neworleansshakespeare.org

The Shakespeare Festival at Tulane is the only professional theater event in the South dedicated to the works of the Bard. Performances take place here every summer. The Lupin Theater also schedules arts in education programs through the year.

5 Mahalia Jackson Theater for the Performing Arts

This 2,243-seat theater *(see p98)*, named for the famous gospel queen, is located on Basin Street. On any given night, the audience can experience top-name artists, the Louisiana Philharmonic Orchestra, Broadway companies, ballet troupes, and other such performers.

6 Contemporary Arts Center New Orleans

Among the many attractions here *(see p80)* is an intimate theater that features musical artists, original stage plays, big-band concerts, and emerging performance artists. The venue is often the setting for cutting-edge performances.

The restored Saenger Theatre

Lady A at Lakefront Arena

7 University of New Orleans Lakefront Arena

6801 Franklin Ave ▪ 504-280-7171
▪ www.arena.uno.edu

The large Lakefront Arena has hosted everything from big-name music artists and sports events to colorful Disney stage productions. Artists such as Christina Aguilera, Lauryn Hill, Arcade Fire, and Common have all taken the stage here.

8 Orpheum Theater

MAP M2 ▪ 129 Roosevelt Way
▪ 504-274-4870 ▪ www.orpheum
nola.com

Located in the revived Theater District, the Orpheum is a favorite venue of the Louisiana Philharmonic Orchestra. In addition to music performances, it stages everything from comedy to burlesque.

9 Smoothie King Center

MAP P1 ▪ 1501 Dave Dixon
Drive ▪ 504-587-3822 ▪ www.
smoothiekingcenter.com

This 17,000-seat facility often hosts sporting events. It also doubles as a venue for artists such as Elton John and the Red Hot Chili Peppers.

10 The AllWays Lounge and Theatre

This comfortable venue (see p100), well loved by the creative types in the city, puts on a wide range of shows, which includes full-scale musicals, stand-up comedy, drag, and burlesque. Regular cabaret shows make for a fun night out. The building also houses the fringe Theatre at St. Claude.

TOP 10 MOVIES THAT WERE FILMED IN NEW ORLEANS

1 A Streetcar Named Desire (1951)
This film, based on Tennessee Williams' play, has stunning performances by Marlon Brando and Vivien Leigh.

2 Pretty Baby (1978)
Twelve-year-old Brooke Shields stars in this controversial picture about Storyville, New Orleans' historic red-light district.

3 Steel Magnolias (1989)
A touching movie about the bond between a group of Southern women.

4 Sex, Lies, and Videotape (1989)
Highly erotic, this movie showed the sultry sensuality of New Orleans.

5 The Pelican Brief (1993)
New Orleans figured prominently in this riveting thriller about a student who uncovers a conspiracy.

6 Interview With a Vampire (1994)
Anne Rice's tale of the vampire Lestat de Lioncourt starred actors Tom Cruise, Brad Pitt, and Kirsten Dunst.

7 Dead Man Walking (1995)
In this crime drama Susan Sarandon plays a New Orleans nun fighting to abolish the death penalty.

8 Ray (2004)
An Academy Award-winning movie on the life of jazz pianist Ray Charles.

9 12 Years a Slave (2013)
One of the most accurate depictions of the evils of American slavery, based on Solomon Northup's searing memoir.

10 Girls Trip (2017)
An emotional comedy on sisterhood and friendship set in New Orleans, especially the French Quarter.

A scene from *Girls Trip* (2017)

⏸10 Live Music Venues

The stage at well-known New Orleans blues club The Howlin' Wolf

① The Howlin' Wolf

This club *(see p82)*, named for bluesman Chester Burnett, or "Howlin' Wolf," is known for attracting big names such as Harry Connick, Jr., Alison Krauss, Foo Fighters, Dr. John, and many more. The unique carved bar is from a hotel once owned by the famed gangster Al Capone. There is also a back room (the Den) that hosts smaller gigs and stand-up comedy shows.

② Candlelight Lounge

One of the few remaining music clubs in Treme, this modest venue *(see p100)* is especially popular for its acclaimed Wednesday night acoustic concerts held by the Treme Brass Band, but the jazz, soul, funk, rap, and R&B is great any night. The menu includes classic Creole dishes.

A band at Candlelight Lounge

③ Maple Leaf Bar

MAP A4 ▪ 8316 Oak St
▪ 504-866-9359

The Maple Leaf Bar attracts an eclectic crowd of college students and people in their 30s and 40s. Big names, such as the Rebirth Brass Band, perform here, but it also promotes upcoming musicians.

④ Pat O'Brien's

Visitors will probably have to wait to get in, but the queue is as much fun as the ambience inside *(see p32)*. The music is lively and the internationally renowned "Hurricane" is the most popular cocktail. The main courtyard has a restaurant and a spectacular fire fountain, which should not be missed.

⑤ Carnaval Lounge

Expect acts toward the punkier end of the scale at this cozy, low-lit venue *(see p100)*, with electronic dance music and the local "bounce" rap featuring strongly, too. It also plays host to drag shows and DJ nights.

⑥ The Spotted Cat Music Club

Some of the city's best jazz musicians regularly play in this intimate venue *(see p100)*, known simply as "The Cat" to many.

7 The Maison

A jazz-oriented line-up is commonly seen at The Maison (see p100), but its three stages allow for a wider variety of acts. The dinner menu and lack of cover charge most nights make it a popular spot, and early arrivals are encouraged. The venue seems pretty large, but the rooms fill up fast.

8 d.b.a.

MAP K6 ■ 618 Frenchman St
■ www.dbaneworleans.com

The stage at this cozy space is usually packed with talent. You are spoiled for choice when it comes to shows at d.b.a., with acts such as brass bands, funk, punk, and rock operas.

Jazz act at local pub Tipitina's

9 Tipitina's

MAP C6 ■ 501 Napoleon Ave
■ 504-895-8477

Named after musician Professor Longhair's recording *Tipitana*, this iconic uptown venue draws some of the hottest jazz and rock acts in Louisiana and from farther afield.

10 Rock 'n' Bowl

This bowling alley (see p106) doubles as a music and dance venue. Go bowling, stay on for a live show and great food, and then dance until the early hours of the morning.

TOP 10 JAZZ CLUBS

Live music at Snug Harbor Jazz Bistro

1 Snug Harbor Jazz Bistro
MAP K6 ■ 626 Frenchmen St
■ 504-949-0696
A jazz musician's club, with decent food.

2 Arnaud's
Live Dixieland jazz (see p95), plus a selected "jazz" menu at a fixed price.

3 Palm Court Jazz Café
MAP L5 ■ 1204 Decatur St
■ 504-525-0200
Live traditional jazz and Creole cuisine.

4 Sweet Lorraine's Jazz Club
MAP K4 ■ 1931 St. Claude Ave
■ 504-945-9654
Great atmosphere, a stellar sound system, and the best jazz in town.

5 Three Muses
This cozy venue (see p101) offers local jazz, small plates, and a great cocktail menu.

6 Preservation Hall
Dedicated to preserving the classic New Orleans jazz tradition (see p33).

7 Fritzel's European Jazz Pub
This intimate jazz hub (see p94) occupies a quiet spot in a busy neighborhood, and has attracted the best musicians since 1969.

8 The Bombay Club
MAP M3 ■ 830 Conti St ■ 504-577-2237
Classy, with live music every weekend.

9 House of Blues
World-renowned musicians play here (see p94). The Gospel Brunch on Sundays is a favorite.

10 Maison Bourbon
MAP L4 ■ 641 Bourbon St ■ 504-522-8818
Popular for its potent mojitos and traditional Southern jazz.

🔟 LGBTQ+ Nightlife

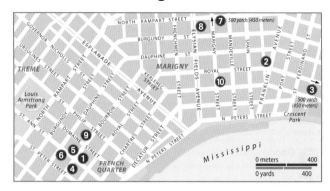

1 Oz
One of the city's most popular dance clubs, Oz *(see p94)* has a vibrant atmosphere, a superb sound system playing high-energy music, and great DJs. There are also several fun weekly events, including Drag Bingo, or "Dingo," "Boy Next Door" contests, themed performances, and daily happy hours from 4 to 8pm. The club is open 24 hours on weekends but Thursday is particularly lively – billed as the "Totally Awesome 80s night," it includes a male strip show at midnight.

The popular dance club, Oz

2 Big Daddy's Bar
Situated slightly off the beaten path in Faubourg Marigny, Big Daddy's *(see p100)* is a small neighborhood lounge bar that is open 24 hours a day, and popular with locals. With an intimate atmosphere, great cocktails, and a pool table, this venue also has some of the friendliest bartenders in New Orleans. A party vibe sets in late at night and lasts until the early hours of the morning.

3 The Country Club
634 Louisa St ▪ 504-945-0742
Housed in an elegant 19th-century Italianate Center Hall mansion in the Bywater neighborhood, The Country Club offers relaxation as well as exciting evening events. Visitors can choose from a number of options, including the restaurant serving Creole South cuisine by executive chef Chris Barbato, a bar, pool, Jacuzzi, spa and massage services, a large movie screen, and cocktails on the veranda. The saltwater pool, hot-tub, and sauna set amid lush greenery are the club's highlights.

4 Napoleon's Itch
**MAP L4 ▪ 734 Bourbon St
▪ 504-371-5450**
Located in Bourbon Street, the center of gay nightlife in New Orleans, Napoleon's Itch is a quiet, upscale bar with a sleek, contemporary interior, and an outdoor area – a perfect place to relax. The impressive drinks menu specializes in a large selection of mojitos and martinis. On Friday and Saturday nights it livens up with dance music.

5 Bourbon Pub Parade

Regarded as the anchor of the LGBTQ+ entertainment district in New Orleans, the Bourbon Pub Parade *(see p32)* is the largest out of the longest continuously operating gay clubs in the U.S. The pub downstairs is constantly packed with patrons watching videos on large screens. Upstairs, the raucous Parade disco area has a dance floor, great DJs, and a variety of live entertainment, including costume contests, cabarets, and male dancers.

6 Good Friends Bar

MAP L4 ▪ 740 Dauphine St ▪ 504-566-7191

A slightly older crowd frequents the warm and welcoming Good Friends Bar. The multi-level venue has a solid mahogany bar downstairs, decorated with custom paintings. Tuesday nights are reserved for karaoke. The Queen's Head Pub upstairs has a wraparound balcony and arranges a piano-bar singalong on Sunday evenings.

Good Friends Bar, an old favorite

7 The AllWays Lounge and Theatre

A fabulous mix of dive bar and performing arts space, the Allways *(see p100)* can always be relied upon for burlesque shows, comedy acts, revues, music, and other varieties of live shows. Whatever alternative theater you're looking for, you're likely to find it here.

8 Phoenix Bar

MAP K6 ▪ 941 Elysian Fields Ave ▪ 504-945-9264

This is one of the most frequented leather bars for the gay community of New Orleans. The Eagle Bar, upstairs, is a popular meeting spot for locals. This place is packed every Friday and Saturday night.

Café Lafitte in Exile

9 Café Lafitte in Exile

MAP L4 ▪ 901 Bourbon St ▪ 504-522-8397

Founded in 1933, this is the oldest gay club in the U.S. and a former haunt of Tennessee Williams and Truman Capote. Today it has two floors of state-of-the-art sound systems and a large video screen. Café Lafitte's balcony is one of the most coveted spots in the city, especially during Mardi Gras. The weekly Wednesday night karaoke and Sunday "Trash Disco" are huge draws.

10 The Friendly Bar

True to its name, The Friendly Bar *(see p100)* has a congenial ambience and friendly bartenders who always greet guests warmly. The DJ plays great music, and the lively pool table and banter make this a great place in which to relax over a beer or cocktail.

TOP 10 Regional Dishes

1 Alligator Sauce Piquante
Traditionally, Cajuns used spicy sauce piquante in dishes made with rabbit. Alligator sauce piquante is a variation that uses the tail meat of an alligator, combined with heavy seasonings, including cayenne pepper, garlic, green chilies, onions, black pepper, and jalapeno peppers.

2 Court Bouillion
A staple in Louisiana Cajun households, court bouillion is essentially a seafood stew, but there are several variations. The two most popular use redfish or catfish. The recipe always features garlic, onion, and celery. Learning to cook this dish requires a lot of practice.

3 Blackened Redfish
Local chef Paul Prudhomme popularized the culinary method of blackening. The redfish recipe calls for the fish to be rubbed with Cajun spices and then cooked on high heat in a cast-iron skillet. The process can be used for chicken, catfish, and other meats and fish.

4 Seafood Gumbo
Gumbo can be safely called the official food of New Orleans (next to red beans and rice, of course). It is a rich, thick dark soup with mixtures of seafood, such as crab, shrimp, catfish, oysters, or whatever the cook desires. Gumbo can also be made using chicken or sausage meat.

5 Jambalaya
Both French and Spanish influences have shaped the jambalaya. This rice-based Creole dish is a bit like paella. Some make it with seafood, while others use chicken, sausages, or both.

Rice-based dish Jambalaya

Tomatoes, celery, and even-handed seasoning are all key to perfecting this dish.

6 Oysters Bienville
Named after the founder of New Orleans, this unique dish was created during the Great Depression at Antoine's, the oldest family-run restaurant in the country. The oysters are topped with sherry, béchamel, cayenne, garlic, shallots, and minced shrimp, and then baked on rock salt with a breadcrumb-and-cheese topping.

A plate of seafood gumbo

7 Fried Green Tomatoes with Shrimp Rémoulade
Green tomatoes have a rich flavor, but in New Orleans the taste is enhanced by frying them in batter and adding fresh Gulf shrimps and tangy rémoulade sauce. A staple dish in the best restaurants of the city.

8 Muffuletta
Legend has it that New Orleans' old Central Grocery was a gathering spot for local workers. Holding bread in one hand and meat in another, they would engage in lively debates, and food would fly. The owner eventually put the meat between slices of bread, added olive salad, and invented the *muffuletta*.

9 Barbecued Shrimp
Not to be confused with foods cooked in bottled barbecue sauces, these shrimps are smoked and then cooked with Worcestershire sauce and black pepper. The best dishes are made with jumbo Gulf shrimps, which are slow cooked. **Barbecued shrimp** The secret to making delicious shrimp is to use a generous amount of real butter.

10 Po' Boys
Sandwiches made of crispy French bread with ingredients such as shrimp, catfish, oysters, beef, ham, crab, and even French fries. Ubiquitous in New Orleans.

A classic po' boy sandwich

TOP 10 DRINKS

Mint Julep, a refreshing cocktail

1 Mint Julep
Iconic in the American South, Mint Juleps are a fragrant mix of bourbon, mint, sugar, and water.

2 Sazerac
Dating from the Civil War, this cocktail contains Cognac, herbsaint (or absinthe), and bitters.

3 Ramos Gin Fizz
Also called New Orleans Fizz, a Ramos Gin Fizz includes gin, lemon, lime, egg white, cream, sugar, and orange-flower water, as well as soda water.

4 Hurricane
This powerful sweet rum drink is the signature cocktail at the French Quarter's Pat O'Brien's bar *(see p32)*.

5 Cajun Martini
Simply adding a shot of jalapeno-infused vodka turns an ordinary martini into a hot and spicy sensation.

6 Mimosa
The Sunday brunch drink of choice is a mixture of fresh orange juice and champagne or sparkling wine.

7 Abita Beer
Brewed in nearby Abita Springs, Louisiana, Abita has eight flagship brews and five seasonal brews.

8 Pimm's Cup
This summery New Orleans favorite is a fruity, gin-based cocktail. It was invented in the mid-19th-century in England as a health tonic.

9 Vieux Carré
This potent whiskey cocktail was first concocted in the Carousel Bar of Hotel Monteleone *(see p29)*.

10 Cajun Bloody Mary
Not just any old Bloody Mary will do – people in New Orleans add hot sauce and horseradish to this classic cocktail.

TOP 10 Cafés

1 HEY! Café & Coffee Roastery

MAP C6 ▪ 4332 Magazine St

Just a cluster of tables are to be found at this cute, cozy café. Patrons come here for the house-roasted coffee, of which numerous varieties from around the world are available, along with a selection of gluten-free pastries. Coffee is served by extremely knowledgeable staff, who also roast the coffee.

2 Vic's Kangaroo Café

MAP P4 ▪ 636 Tchoupitoulas St
▪ 504-524-4329

Known for its beers on tap, Vic's is usually loud and crowded owing to its friendly vibe and attentive service. Excellent Australian specialties are featured on the menu.

3 Café du Monde

Since 1862, locals have relied on Café du Monde for their morning coffee with chicory and beignets (fried pastries with powdered sugar), a New Orleans specialty. The café has multiple locations, but the anchor restaurant is the one in the city's French Quarter. Be sure to snag an outdoor table, where you can relax while listening to street musicians entertaining the crowds.

4 Stein's

This bustling Jewish deli (see p76) not only makes some of the city's finest hot and cold sandwiches but also serves great coffees and sweet treats. Desserts include cheesecakes, brownies, and chocolate chip cookies.

5 Café Amelie

Weekend brunch at Café Amelie (see p29) is served in its beautiful courtyard. Everything on the menu is expertly executed, and the ambience is second to none. Highlights include crab cakes with a citrus drizzle, vegetable pasta, and the blackened catfish sandwich.

6 Z'otz

MAP A4 ▪ 8210 Oak St
▪ www.zotzcafe.com

This is the sort of funky, artsy café that could be a movie set in a film. It has quirky interiors and features unique artwork. The coffee is excellent.

Café du Monde

Diners enjoying a meal at Café Degas

7 Café Degas

For a true French café experience, head to Café Degas *(see p107)*. The restaurant offers everything from a light hors d'oeuvres menu and a stellar French onion soup, to perfectly cooked steak frites.

8 Napoleon House

Serving legendary mufuletta Italian sandwiches and desserts, Napoleon House *(see p95)* is an atmospheric European-style café. The building dates from 1798 and was originally intended as a residence for the French emperor in exile.

9 Petite Clouet

MAP F3 ▪ 3100 Royal St

This café in the Bywater neighborhood lives up to its name – it is tiny but is nonetheless an excellent place to people watch while sipping freshly brewed coffee. The breakfast menu of tacos and baked goods is great.

10 Who Dat Coffee Café

MAP F3 ▪ 2401 Burgundy St
▪ 504-872-0360

This small but lively local hangout, located in the Marigny neighborhood, serves delicious coffee. Don't miss out on the tasty jalapeno corn bread.

TOP 10 BREAKFAST SPOTS

1 Willa Jean
MAP E4 ▪ 611 O'Keefe Ave
▪ 504-509-7334
Hearty Southern classics and some lighter fare are served at this airy café.

2 Satsuma Café
A hip, friendly local diner *(see p101)* serving healthy breakfast options.

3 SoBou
MAP M4 ▪ 310 Chartres St
▪ 504-552-4095
A slick restaurant with a Creole menu, plus a burlesque brunch on Sundays.

4 Poydras & Peters
Try the breakfast *banh mi* (Vietnamese sandwich) or pancakes *(see p85)* here.

5 Brennan's
Bananas Foster and Eggs Sardou have been served here *(see p95)* since 1946.

6 Eat New Orleans
MAP L4 ▪ 900 Dumaine St
▪ 504-522-7222
From the grillades to the fresh bagels, breakfast here is hearty and filling.

7 Slim Goodies Diner
MAP G6 ▪ 3322 Magazine St
▪ 504-891-3447
This place offers hearty eggs, meat, and potatoes breakfasts. Cash only.

8 The Camellia Grill
The omelets here *(see p61)* are made fresh and grilled in front of guests.

9 The Ruby Slipper Café
MAP M3 ▪ 2001 Burgundy St
▪ 504-525-9355
The Marigny branch of a popular diner.

10 Mother's
MAP P4 ▪ 401 Poydras St
▪ 504-523-9656
Enjoy eggs cooked any style and fresh biscuits with meat to start the day.

A prawn dish at Mother's

🔟 Restaurants

The serene, leafy surroundings of refined restaurant Commander's Palace

① Commander's Palace
Known for impeccable service and gracious ambience, Commander's (see p77) excels with the house turtle soup, fresh seafood, and its signature bread pudding soufflé. Ask for a table in the Garden Room.

② La Petite Grocery
Chef Justin Devillier was named the Best Chef: South at the 2016 James Beard Awards, thanks to stand-out dishes including blue crab beignets and turtle bolognese. The traditional New Orleans cuisine (see p77) is served in a century-old building that has previously housed a coffee and tea depot, grocery store, butcher shop, and florist.

③ Compère Lapin
Housed in the hip Old No. 77 Hotel, this popular spot (see p85) by chef Nina Compton has received rave reviews for its unique melting pot of Caribbean, French, Italian, and Creole cuisines. The ever-changing menu has diverse dishes such as cold smoked tuna tartare and curried goat with sweet potato gnocchi.

④ August
Upscale and elegant, this downtown restaurant (see p85) features creative dishes such as roasted swordfish with wild mushrooms, and a tasting of vegetables from the farmers market. Local, seasonal ingredients are the stars on the menu by chef Ross Dover.

⑤ Arnaud's
This restaurant (see p95) has served the city since 1918. Featuring both classic and innovative Creole dishes, the menu is matched by the elegant ambience and exemplary service. Shrimp Arnaud, oysters Bienville, and market fish meunière are among the specialties offered here.

Dish of oysters at Arnaud's

⑥ Atchafalaya
Brunch is served from Thursday to Monday at this intimate uptown spot (see p77). Its Bloody Mary bar and mouthwatering Creole menu attracts locals looking for Louisiana specialties, such as boudin cake. Dinner is a romantic affair, with dimly lit dining rooms on two levels and a creative menu that doesn't feel pretentious.

7 Dooky Chase

During her long career, Leah Chase *(see p107)* has won every culinary award possible, and she still plays a part in ensuring that her fried chicken is world-class. Even former President Obama dined here. Locals navigate the unusual opening hours to sit down with a plate of heaven.

8 Mr. B's Bistro

Anchoring the corner of Royal and Bienville streets in the French Quarter, this casually elegant bistro *(see p29)* prepares dishes such as Gumbo Ya-Ya (made with chicken and spicy sausage) and a honey-ginger glazed pork chop. Sunday brunch is a treat: try the barbecued shrimp.

9 Brigtsen's

Frank Brigtsen worked in some of New Orleans' finest kitchens before opening his own award-winning Creole restaurant *(see p77)* in a quaint uptown house. Enjoy hearty comfort food dishes such as roasted duck and sesame-crusted rabbit with spinach.

10 Shaya

This bright, stylish spot *(see p77)* serves high-end Israeli food. The rush to reserve a table was already in full swing by the time the restaurant won Best New Restaurant in the U.S. in 2016. Head over for lunch, when crowds are less intense.

High-end dining at Shaya

TOP 10 PLACES FOR LATE-NIGHT DINING

The interior of Clover Grill

1 Clover Grill
Burgers and breakfast dishes are always on the menu at this 24-hour restaurant *(see p33)*.

2 Junction
MAP K4 ▪ 3021 St. Claude Ave ▪ www.junctionnola.com ▪ $
This place serves a variety of delicious burgers and good beer.

3 Port of Call
Great burgers and cocktails *(see p101)*.

4 NOLA Poboys & Bar
MAP K6 ▪ 517 Frenchmen St ▪ $
This laid-back bar serves huge po'boys.

5 The Camellia Grill
MAP A4 ▪ 626 S. Carrollton Ave ▪ 504-309-2679 ▪ $
Sit at the counter for fried apple pie, cheeseburgers, and crispy French fries.

6 Igor's
MAP D5 ▪ 2133 St. Charles Ave ▪ 504-568-9811 ▪ $
Enjoy burgers at this all-hours dive bar.

7 Ernst Café
MAP P4 ▪ 600 S. Peters St ▪ 504-525-8544 ▪ $$
Sophisticated bar food includes crawfish stew and gumbo.

8 Turtle Bay
MAP L5 ▪ 1119 Decatur St ▪ 504-586-0563 ▪ $$
Enjoy pizza, burgers, and icy Abita beer.

9 Avenue Pub
MAP R2 ▪ 1732 St. Charles Ave ▪ 504-586-9243 ▪ $$
Excellent beers and a solid kitchen make this a popular late-night choice.

10 Buffa's
This nightspot *(see p101)* offers great burgers, chicken wings, and often live music to boot.

TOP 10 Shops and Markets

Entrance to Canal Place

1 Canal Place

This multipurpose center *(see p36)* on the edge of the French Quarter offers theaters, cafés, restaurants, and upscale retailers. Shoppers can easily spend a whole day browsing stores such as the multilevel Saks Fifth Avenue, Pottery Barn, Coach, and Brooks Brothers.

2 Mignon Faget

Original jewelry items designed by Mignon Faget are on sale in this store *(see p76)*. Her elegant and sometimes quirky designs are inspired by the natural surroundings and human-made structures of New Orleans. The store also stocks beautiful home-decor pieces, including glassware, linens, and baby gifts.

3 Adler's

Around since 1898, Adler's *(see p84)* has been the top jeweler in New Orleans for over a century. The firm is still owned by the family that founded it, and buyers from around the world come here to find unique pieces. They have an extensive giftware line, as well as a range of locally inspired items, including New Orleans-themed holiday ornaments and Mardi Gras jewelry.

4 Rubensteins

Since 1924, Rubensteins *(see p37)* has been one of the most respected purveyors of menswear in New Orleans. Detailed tailoring as well as personal attention define the service here.

5 Fifi Mahony's

In New Orleans, you could easily need a last-minute wig for a spontaneous costume party, and this funky French Quarter boutique *(see p93)* is just the place. Experienced staff take you through the fitting.

6 Trashy Diva

MAP S3 ■ 2048 Magazine St ■ 504-299-8777

This boutique specializes in colorful fitted dresses with eye-catching patterns. There's a wide selection of garments, from special-occasion cocktail dresses to everyday wear with a vintage flavor. Next door, its sister stores sell equally fabulous lingerie and shoes.

Dress from Trashy Diva

7 Fleur de Paris

Housed in a historic building, Fleur de Paris *(see p29)* is known internationally for its custom millinery and couture gowns. European-trained milliners create exquisite one-of-a-kind hats on site, with antique flowers, feathers, veiling, and silk ribbons.

Renowned milliner Fleur de Paris

⑧ KREWE
MAP L5 ■ **809 Royal St**
■ 504-684-2939

A tropical climate with year-round sunshine demands stylish sun glasses, and this boutique has an exciting range of styles inspired by the diverse cultures of the city. The frames are made from high-quality plastics, and everything from the hinges to the lenses is engineered with care, making for highly desirable pieces.

Shoppers at the French Market

⑨ The French Market
On the edge of the Mississippi River, the picturesque French Market (see p90) is a conglomeration of an outdoor farmers' market, a covered flea market, shops, arts and crafts boutiques, and restaurants. The lively market is also the site of a number of special events, jazz concerts, and festivals that take place throughout the year.

⑩ The Outlet Collection at Riverwalk
Local businesses and national retailers blend nicely in this large waterfront complex (see p23). The mall, built on the site of the 1984 Louisiana World Exposition (see p41), offers tax-free shopping for inter-national visitors looking for small souvenirs, clothing, decor items, and the latest high-tech games. There are also several restaurants, bars, and fast food joints.

TOP 10 SOUVENIRS AND KEEPSAKES

Traditional ceramic masks

1 Ceramic Masks
The tradition of Mardi Gras masking is enshrined in locally made ceramic masks. A wonderful holiday keepsake.

2 Mardi Gras Beads
Although they are usually made of plastic, the colorful Mardi Gras beads that are caught from float-riders are considered as precious as gold.

3 Voodoo Dolls
These exquisitely detailed figures are sold at stores all over the city. They are colorful representations of the local voodoo tradition.

4 Bourbon Street T-Shirts
There are souvenir T-shirt shops on most blocks in the French Quarter.

5 New Orleans Coffee Beans
The best local coffees are made by Community Coffee and Luzianne, and are sold all over the city.

6 Jambalaya Mix
A great way to take home a taste of New Orleans is with the Cajun food producer Zatarain's jambalaya mix.

7 Red Beans and Rice Mix
Delicious and easy to make, red beans and rice make up the official "Monday night dish" in New Orleans.

8 Cajun Spices
Chefs such as Emeril Lagasse and others take pride in their secret spice mixtures, available for sale citywide.

9 Pat O'Brien's Hurricane Glass
Pat O'Brien's bar (see p32) mixes powerful "Hurricane" drinks. Guests even get to keep the glass.

10 Restaurant Cookbooks
The best chefs in town have their own cookbooks, which are usually for sale in their restaurants.

🔟 New Orleans for Free

1 New Orleans Parks

Retreat from the hustle and bustle of the city to one of the many parks in New Orleans. Enjoy a walk in the New Orleans City Park (see pp16–17) or stroll along the riverfront at Woldenberg Park (see p22).

2 Stand-up Comedy

The comedy scene in New Orleans is always growing, and visitors can see stand-up shows featuring local and touring comedians for free every night of the week. The best are at The Howlin' Wolf (see p52) on Tuesday nights, and the AllWays Lounge and Theatre (see p51) on Saturday nights.

3 Commemorate History

Chalmette Battlefield: Jean Lafitte National Historical Park, 8606 West St. Bernard Highway, Chalmette; 504-281-0510; www.nps. gov/jela ■ Navy Week: www.nola navyweek.com

New Orleans' turbulent history is commemorated in many ways, and its various battles to retain its identity are remembered. The anniversary of the Battle of New Orleans, in January, sees a huge reenactment at Chalmette Battlefield. During Navy Week, in April, historic tall ships line the shores of the Mississippi along the Warehouse District, the French Quarter, and the Marigny.

Masked reveler at Mardi Gras

4 Mardi Gras

Across the city ■ www.mardi grasneworleans.com

The biggest free party rocks all of New Orleans with a month or so of parades and parties all over the city, culminating on the big day itself. Look at the schedule and see which parades take your fancy – there's everything from miniature floats to dogs in costume.

5 Mini Music Festivals

Summers are long in New Orleans, but the city rewards those who brave the heat with a choice of mini music festivals that last just one evening. The various series run at Louis Armstrong Park (see p97), Lafayette Square (see p82), and Algiers Point on the West Bank, and involve many big local names.

6 Museums for Free

St. Mary's Assumption Church: MAP J5; 923 Josephine St; 504-522-6748 ■ Germaine Cazenave Wells Mardi Gras Museum: MAP M3; Arnaud's, 813 Bienville St (enter via restaurant); 504-523–5433; www. arnaudsrestaurant.com/about/ mardi-gras-museum

New Orleans is a living museum in many ways, but visitors can also discover more detailed information about its history. Try The Historic New Orleans Collection (see p90), St. Mary's Assumption Church, and the Germaine Cazenave Wells Mardi Gras Museum for a look at the diverse aspects of the city.

Tall ships on the Mississippi during Navy Week

7 Learn to Dance
MAP K4 ▪ 2358 St. Claude Ave
▪ 504-383-5284 ▪ www.nola.com

New Orleans has a wealth of wonderful music on offer, but, to get into the swing of things, it pays to know how to dance. NOLA Jitterbugs Dance School hosts a choice of free dance lessons at venues around the city. Beginners are always welcome.

8 Street Parades
New Orleans comes alive during its huge festive parades at holiday time. There's spooky pageantry, dazzling costumes, and impressive parades during Halloween. On St. Patrick's Day, the city's American-Irish population celebrates with Mardi Gras-style parades. For Juneteenth celebrations, the passionate Second Lines parades marching the neighborhoods are unmissable.

Jazz performance, French Quarter

9 Jazz on Frenchmen Street
MAP K6 ▪ Frenchmen St

The Frenchmen Street clubs usually charge a cover fee, but you won't be charged for enjoying music through open doors and perusing the carnivalesque street markets.

10 NOLA Brewery Tours
MAP R4 ▪ 3001 Tchoupitoulas St ▪ 504-896-9996 ▪ Tours: 2–3pm Fri, 2– 4pm Sat & Sun ▪ www.nolabrewing.com

Go behind the scenes during free tours of the NOLA brewery on Friday and Saturday afternoons. The free samples are a popular part of the tour.

TOP 10 BUDGET TIPS

Streetcars in New Orleans

1 Public transport – both buses and streetcars – is very cheap, so it's worth making the most of it. Riding the streetcar a fun experience in itself.

2 Visitors can buy a good-value Jazzy Pass for cheaper fares, with 1-, 3-, and 30-day passes available.

3 Many restaurants and bars have a happy hour around 4–6pm, often with some very good deals including cocktails and small plates.

4 Look in unusual places for free concerts, from St. Louis Cathedral (see p90) to the Old U.S. Mint (see p92). Many bars have regular live performances with no cover charge – just walk around and keep your eyes and ears open.

5 Take the ferry instead of a cruise for a riverside view of the city skyline.

6 Visit during the low season, which runs from June to September. December and January can also be quiet months, but that is just before the madness of Mardi Gras sets in.

7 Plan well ahead for Mardi Gras and major festivals such as Jazz Fest. Prices spike as they approach.

8 Go for a walk. Most neighborhoods in the city are compact enough that visitors do not have to use taxis; besides, the best way to admire the unique architecture of the area is by setting out on foot.

9 Take a free tour of the French Quarter, run by Free Tours by Foot. Bookings can be made online (www.freetoursbyfoot.com).

10 In season, many bars host crawfish or shrimp boils, and you can eat for a small set price.

🔟 Festivals and Events

① Mardi Gras

New Orleans is internationally known for its Carnival celebrations that gear up about three weeks before Lent. Mardi Gras *(see pp34–5)* itself draws a million tourists each year for street parties, parades, and masked balls. The more risqué side of Carnival happens in the French Quarter, while family celebrations happen in neighborhoods all over town.

Parade at Jazz and Heritage Festival

② French Quarter Festival

504-522-5730 ▪ www.fqfi.org

Every April, for one weekend, the French Quarter turns into a 15-square-block street party. Stages are set up all over the Quarter and top jazz, rock, hip-hop, and Cajun bands play to huge audiences. In Jackson Square and the nearby Woldenberg Park local restaurants serve their signature drinks and dishes from makeshift booths.

③ New Orleans Wine and Food Experience (NOWFE)

504-529-9463 ▪ www.nowfe.com

During the NOWFE, held every April, local restaurants host vintner dinners, while daytime hours are spent in seminars, and at cooking demos. The festival culminates with the Grand Tasting, where attendees can meet top chefs.

④ Jazz and Heritage Festival

504-410-4100 ▪ www.nojazzfest.com

Covering two weekends in April and May, the locally dubbed "Jazz Fest" offers top performers from all over the world in jazz, gospel, Cajun, R&B, zydeco (Louisiana Creole Blues and R&B), blues, rock, funk, African, and Latin music. Look for local crafters displaying their wares and foods.

⑤ Creole Tomato Festival

Tomatoes have long been an essential crop in Louisiana. Every June, the French Market *(see p90)* hosts a festival dedicated to this fruit with cooking demos, art exhibits, music and dancing, as well as the crowning of the Tomato Queen.

The popular New Orleans Wine and Food Experience

⑥ Go Fourth on the River
www.go4thontheriver.com

Barges on the Mississippi River offer spectacular fireworks choreographed in time to stirring patriotic music on Independence Day (July 4).

⑦ ESSENCE Festival
www.essence.com/festival

African-American culture is celebrated on the Independence Day weekend every year with the ESSENCE Festival. This showcases big-name performers, African-American artists, writers, crafters, culinary artists, and others.

⑧ Satchmo Summerfest
504-522-5730 ▪ www.fqfi.org

In early August each year one of the city's favorite sons, Louis "Satchmo" Armstrong, is honored with a festival in his name. One of the pre-eminent jazz musicians of the 20th century, Armstrong is heralded with live jazz, seminars, and all-day partying.

Celebrations at Satchmo Summerfest

⑨ Southern Decadence
www.southerndecadence.net

One of the largest LGBTQ+ events in the U.S. takes place in the French Quarter every September. The weekend includes a huge costume parade, drag shows, parties, and more.

⑩ Christmas
504-522-5730 ▪ www.fqfi.org

Christmas is celebrated across New Orleans with a number of events: concerts at St. Louis Cathedral, gospel performances, Christmas carols in Jackson Square, and special menus at French Quarter restaurants.

TOP 10 OTHER FESTIVALS AND EVENTS

Halloween New Orleans™

1 Tennessee Williams Literary Festival
Held in late March, the festival includes panel discussions, theater, and food.

2 Ponchatoula Strawberry Festival
A short drive from New Orleans, Ponchatoula hosts a festival featuring music, games, strawberry-eating, and cooking contests every April.

3 Greek Festival
This May event features live Greek music, traditional cuisine, a marketplace, and family-friendly activities.

4 Shakespeare Festival
The Bard is honored annually (May–Jul) at Tulane University with performances of his most famous works (see p50).

5 Tales of the Cocktail
The history and culture of the cocktail is the centerpiece of this annual July event.

6 Whitney White Linen Night
White linen attire is worn during this annual August street party, held in the city's Warehouse District.

7 Beignet Fest
Try the different types of the famous pillowy donuts, along with live music and other family fun at this fiesta.

8 Halloween New Orleans™
Every Halloween, the city's LGBTQ+ community sponsors a fun-filled party weekend to benefit Lazarus House, an AIDS hospice.

9 Voodoo Music Festival
A Halloween weekend of rock, jazz, and hip hop held every year at New Orleans City Park (see pp16–17).

10 Oak Street Po-Boy Festival
Celebrate the ubiquitous po'boy with live music at this local-favorite festival, held in mid-November.

TOP 10 Excursions and Day Trips

Oak trees in front of the Oak Alley Plantation

① Oak Alley Plantation

MAP B2 ▪ 3645 Highway 18, Vacherie ▪ 225-265-2151 ▪ Open 9am–4:30pm Mon–Fri (to 5pm Sat & Sun) ▪ Adm ▪ www.oakalleyplantation.com

The setting for many major movies and television shows, Oak Alley is a striking plantation property. A canopy of giant oak trees forms an impressive avenue that leads to a Greek Revival-style mansion.

② St. Martin's Parish

www.cajuncountry.org

A trip to Louisiana would not be complete without a day spent in Cajun Country. Located in the Atchafalaya Basin, St. Martin's Parish and its surrounding towns form part of a national heritage area. A little over two hours' drive west of New Orleans, this region is rich in history and is home to traditional Cajun and Creole cuisine.

③ St. Martinville

MAP A1 ▪ www.stmartinville.org

With a small population of only 7,000 residents, St. Martinville retains its small-town flavor and Southern charm. Every February, the town hosts La Grande Boucherie des Cajuns, which celebrates Cajun culture with feasting and games. The town is also home to an African-American museum, which traces the history of slavery in the region.

④ Whitney Plantation

MAP B1 ▪ 5099 Louisiana Highway 18, Edgard ▪ 225-265-3300 ▪ Open 9:30am–4:30pm Wed–Mon ▪ Adm ▪ www.whitneyplantation.com

Slavery and the lives of the enslaved are in focus at this museum, located within a former plantation. On display are sculptures, restored rooms, and first-person narratives.

5 Laura Plantation
MAP A1 ■ 2247 Hwy 18, Vacherie ■ Open 10am–4pm daily ■ Adm ■ www.lauraplantation.com

Built in 1805, Laura gained renown for the stories told by the French-speaking enslaved African people, later tenant farmers, who lived there. These tales were translated by folklorist Alcée Fortier in the late 19th century and are today famous as the Br'er Rabbit stories. Guided tours explore the history of the plantation and a permanent exhibition is dedicated to telling the story of the enslaved community who lived and worked here.

The Laura Plantation house

6 River Road
MAP B2

Often called the Great River Road, this stretch between New Orleans and Baton Rouge is home to carefully preserved plantation houses and museums dedicated to the history of these buildings as well as that of the enslaved peoples who built them.

7 Baton Rouge
MAP B1 ■ www.visit batonrouge.com

Louisiana's capital city is worth the hour-long drive from New Orleans. Baton Rouge is a metropolis with great dining and a buzzing nightlife. Visitors can also enjoy boat tours of the river, swamp tours, riverboat casinos, and museums, and visit beautiful vineyards.

A statue in St. Francisville

A traditional property in Lafayette

8 Lafayette
MAP A1 ■ www.lafayette travel.com

Although it is a four-hour drive from New Orleans, Lafayette is a popular weekend getaway. Located in the heart of Cajun Country, this city has a very distinct culture and offers visitors many attractions, including eclectic local cuisine, a national park, and a buzzing nightlife.

9 Biloxi
www.biloxi.ms.us

An hour's drive from New Orleans, this once-sleepy town has developed into the casino capital of the Gulf Coast. Today, high-rise hotels, big-name entertainers, and flashy casinos are the big draw, not to mention the lovely beaches and exquisite homes and condominiums. The town also offers some of the best sport fishing in the region, and is famous for its delicious seafood.

10 St. Francisville
MAP A1 ■ www. stfrancisville.us

Time stands still in this small and elegant town, with its historic mansions and gorgeous 19th-century gardens. Pleasant bed and breakfasts, restaurants, art galleries, and specialty shops are the attractions of this typical Southern town.

New Orleans
Area by Area

The New Orleans skyline at night

🔟 Garden District and Uptown

Developed on what was once plantation land, uptown New Orleans extends over a large part of the city and was founded by the settlers who built commercial properties and houses here. The Garden District was established in 1832 on the Livaudais Plantation, where wealthy merchants, bankers, and planters built grand mansions surrounded by lush gardens, giving the area its name. This neighborhood is distinguished by its beautiful landscaping and provides a retreat from the urban cityscape. A great way to experience these districts is by taking a streetcar ride from the Central Business District to the top of Uptown. A large part of the Garden District is a National Historic Landmark District, and

visitors can explore the parks, historic buildings, and quaint antiques shops of this neighborhood entirely on foot.

White wood storks at Audubon Zoo

GARDEN DISTRICT AND UPTOWN

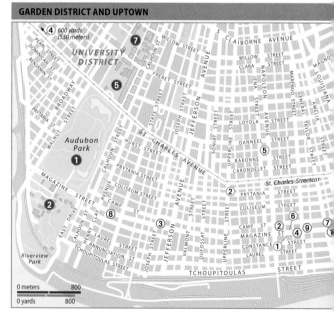

A bucolic scene at a lakeside pavilion in Audubon Park

① Audubon Park
MAP A5 ■ 6500 Magazine St
■ 504-861-2537 ■ www.audubon
natureinstitute.org

With its jogging paths, elegant fountains, and golf course, Audubon Park is the centerpiece of the Uptown area. Named for wildlife painter John James Audubon, it is a favorite haunt of local bird-watchers, who are likely to see egrets and several species of duck, among others. A golf clubhouse offers refreshments.

② Audubon Zoo
MAP A6 ■ 6500 Magazine St
■ 504-581-4629 ■ Open 10am–5pm
Mon–Fri (to 6pm Sat & Sun) ■ Adm
■ www.audubonnatureinstitute.org

This popular zoo is home to a large number of animals from all over the globe and is dedicated to preserving the various species in its care. The emphasis is on interactive exhibits – the award-winning Louisiana Swamp exhibit is one of the most engaging. Although the zoo's focus is on children's attractions, the overall experience is so enjoyable that it appeals to visitors of all age groups.

The iconic St. Charles streetcar

③ St. Charles Streetcar
MAP B5 ■ 504-827-8300
■ Adm ■ www.norta.com

Streetcars are as much a part of the city's character as its architecture, and the St. Charles streetcar is the most famous. The vintage green tram runs for 7 miles (11 km) along St. Charles Avenue, from downtown Canal Street to Uptown Carrollton Avenue, through the Central Business District. It has featured in movies, paintings, and novels.

GARDEN DISTRICT

Cornstalk fence at Colonel Short's Villa

4 Colonel Short's Villa
MAP H5 ■ 1448 4th St

Built in 1859 for Colonel Robert Short of Kentucky, this is one of the most stunning historic homes in the Garden District. Designed by architect Henry Howard, the house is known for its cornstalk fence and is a favorite stop on walking tours.

5 Loyola University
MAP B5 ■ 6363 St. Charles Ave
■ 504-865-3240 ■ www.loyno.edu

A Jesuit institution that was declared a university in 1912, Loyola University is spread over two campuses on either side of St. Charles Avenue. With nearly 3,000 students, this is one of the largest private Catholic universities in the South. It offers degrees in many academic disciplines and is also home to the well-respected Thelonious Monk Institute of Jazz Performance. Loyola's imposing Tudor-Gothic architecture is symbolized by the Marquette Hall, one of the grandest buildings on campus.

**Marquette Hall at
Loyola University**

6 Toby's Corner
MAP H5 ■ 2340 Prytania St

A stroll through the Garden District reveals a proliferation of houses built in the Greek-Revival style. Among these is Toby's Corner, built around 1838 and believed to be the oldest house in the city. Named for wealthy merchant Thomas Toby and striking in its simplicity, this suburban villa is raised on brick piers in classic Creole style, to allow air to circulate underneath and to avoid flooding. The grounds also have a fountain fashioned out of a large sugar kettle.

7 Tulane University
MAP B5 ■ 6823 St. Charles Ave
■ 504-865-5000 ■ St. Charles streetcar
■ www.tulane.edu

One of the best-known local colleges, Tulane University is a private institution that dates back to the early 1800s. Consistently ranked among the top 50 educational institutions in the U.S., the university is easily identified from St. Charles Avenue by the Romanesque Gibson Hall, constructed in 1894.

8 Robinson House
MAP H5 ■ 1415 3rd St

Robinson House was the first house in New Orleans to feature indoor plumbing. Architect Henry Howard constructed a roof that served as a cistern. Gravity pushed the water down, providing adequate water pressure indoors. Also unique to this home is the Italian villa-style architecture, not commonly found in the South. Another original feature is the fact that the side of the house faces the street.

LOYOLA

GARDEN DISTRICT ARCHITECTURE

Three architectural styles dominate the Garden District area. Double-gallery houses are two-story structures with front-facing galleries on each level; 19th-century townhouses are narrow three-story buildings with balconies on the second floor; and the raised center-hall cottages are one-and-a-half- story structures resting on brick piers.

⑨ Briggs-Staub House
MAP H5 ■ 2605 Prytania St

Briggs-Staub House was built in 1849 for Londoner Charles Briggs, who insisted that his home be referred to as a "Gothic Cottage." He appointed architect James Gallier Sr. to design his home. The style was adhered to on the exterior, but, inside, the rooms are larger than one would expect to find in a typical Gothic-Revival house.

Gothic-Revival Briggs-Staub House

⑩ Lafayette Cemetery No. 1
MAP H5 ■ 1400 Washington Ave ■ 504-525-3377 ■ Open 7am–3pm Mon–Fri, 8am–4pm Sat ■ Adm for tours ■ www.saveourcemeteries.org

New Orleans is technically below sea level, so its citizens are buried in above-ground tombs and vaults. This walled cemetery was laid out in 1833, its lavish tombs decorated in accordance with the ornate architecture of the Garden District. The best way to see the cemetery and learn about its rich history is through daily guided tours (booked online).

A WALK AROUND THE GARDEN DISTRICT

▶ MORNING

Start your day with poached eggs, crab cakes, and fried green tomatoes at **Atchafalaya** *(see p77)*, a popular place serving creative Louisiana cuisine. Next, head northwest to Magazine Street, which has some of the city's best antiques shops and galleries. Browse artworks in a lovely minimalist space at the **Cole Pratt Gallery** *(see p76)*, then step into **Mignon Faget**, opposite, to admire beautifully handcrafted jewelry. Explore the multitude of tempting stores as you wander down the street to the heart of the Garden District. Bounded by Magazine Street and Louisiana, Charles, and Jackson avenues, this historic neighborhood is one of the city's most charming. Make sure you join a tour of the district or of **Lafayette Cemetery No. 1** – guides will bring the area to life.

AFTERNOON

After the tour, head to **Commander's Palace** *(see p77)* for lunch. Be sure to try the signature turtle soup and Creole bread pudding soufflé. After lunch, stroll around the area, admiring its grand mansions, including **Colonel Short's Villa**, **Robinson House**, and **Briggs-Staub House**. Then head toward St. Charles Avenue. Admire the famous **St. Charles streetcar** *(see p73)* and take in the grand facades of the buildings on this street as you walk to **Emeril's Delmonico** *(see p77)* for cocktails and a selection of small plates.

See map on pp72–3 ⬅

Shopping

1 Cole Pratt Gallery
MAP C6 ■ 3800 Magazine St
■ 504-891-6789 ■ www.colepratt
gallery.com

This contemporary fine art gallery specializes in Southern artists. The works are displayed in an elegant minimalist space.

Contemporary art at Cole Pratt Gallery

2 Uptown Costume & Dancewear
MAP H6 ■ 4326 Magazine St
■ 504-895-7969

In New Orleans, there's always a need for a special costume. If you'd like to dress up with the locals, head to this overflowing store for a mask, feather boa, or a steampunk ensemble.

3 Hazelnut
MAP B6 ■ 5525 Magazine St
■ 504-891-2424

This interior design store is worth a trip for visitors, as it also sells a range of gifts that you won't find elsewhere in town. You may also catch one of the owners, *Mad Men* star Bryan Batt.

4 Villa Vici
MAP C6 ■ 4112 Magazine St ■ 504-899-2931

Well-known interior designer Vikki Leftwich offers innovative lighting, avant-garde furniture, and fine fabrics at her store. This is a great one-stop shop for home decor.

Armchair from Villa Vici

5 The Renaissance Shop
MAP J5 ■ 2104 Magazine St
■ 504-525-8568

Fine antique reproductions, expert upholstery, and meticulous furniture repair are this shop's specialties.

6 Belladonna Day Spa + Retail Therapy
MAP H6 ■ 2900 Magazine St
■ 504-891-4393

This two-story space houses an elegant personal-care and home accessories store on the ground floor and a world-class spa upstairs.

7 Mignon Faget
MAP C6 ■ 3801 Magazine St
■ 504-891-2005

An upscale designer jewelry store, Mignon Faget creates beautiful custom-created and specially hand-crafted pieces inspired by New Orleans culture and landscapes.

8 Perlis
MAP B6 ■ 6070 Magazine St
■ 504-895-8661

Since 1939, Perlis has been the clothier of choice for many New Orleans families. The store offers casual wear for men, women, and children. It also has a rental and sales division for formal wear.

9 Weinstein's
MAP C6 ■ 4011 Magazine St
■ 504-895-6278

Weinstein's stocks fine European fashion items for women and an array of upscale designer brands for both men and women.

10 Fleurty Girl
MAP H6 ■ 3137 Magazine St ■ 504-309-3944

Souvenirs with the NOLA theme and slogan T-shirts find space alongside clothing and accessories by local designers, on the racks of this cute shop.

Places to Eat

PRICE CATEGORIES

For a three-course meal for one, with half a bottle of wine (or equivalent meal), taxes, and extra charges.

$ under $25 $$ $25–$50 $$$ over $50

1 La Petite Grocery
MAP C6 ■ 4238 Magazine St ■ 504-891-3377 ■ $$$

Chef and owner Justin Devillier took over after helping to rebuild this elegant restaurant (see p60) post-Hurricane Katrina. New Orleans dishes with a modern twist include blue crab beignets.

2 Upperline
MAP C6 ■ 1413 Upperline St ■ 504-891-9822 ■ $$$

A massive art collection is on display here. Do not miss the sensational fried green tomatoes served with shrimp rémoulade.

3 Coquette
MAP H6 ■ 2800 Magazine St ■ 504-265-0421 ■ $$$

With a menu focusing on farm-to-table cuisine, Coquette looks like a chic Parisian bistro. All items are offered in both small plate and entrée size. The grilled shrimp and smoked catfish are excellent.

4 Brigtsen's
MAP A4 ■ 723 Dante St ■ 504-861-7610 ■ $$$

Intimate dining rooms decorated with murals make this place (see p61) a romantic uptown choice. Housed in a Victorian Creole cottage, Brigtsen's serves renowned gumbo and seafood.

5 Pascal's Manale
MAP C5 ■ 1838 Napoleon Ave ■ 504-895-4877 ■ $$$

The barbecued shrimp, an iconic local favorite, is a specialty at Pascal's Manale, opened in 1913. Today, the restaurant still uses the same recipe it devised in the 1950s. It also offers other seafood and Italian dishes.

6 Shaya
MAP C6 ■ 4213 Magazine St ■ 504-891-4213 ■ $$$

At Shaya (see p61), simple Israeli and Mediterranean dishes, such as hummus and tabouleh, are prepared elegantly and with superb ingredients.

7 Stein's
MAP J5 ■ 2207 Magazine St ■ 504-527-0771 ■ $

This busy deli has lines out the door waiting on delicious pastrami-on-rye sandwiches and a well-stocked beer fridge. It's both eat-in and takeout.

8 Commander's Palace
MAP H5 ■ 1403 Washington Ave ■ 504-899-8221 ■ $$$

This historic restaurant (see p60) is the grande dame of New Orleans fine dining. Creole cuisine at its very best.

Elegant room at Emeril's Delmonico

9 Emeril's Delmonico
MAP R2 ■ 1300 St. Charles Ave ■ 504-525-4937 ■ $$$

At the most upscale of Emeril's chain of restaurants, diners can sample Chef Anthony Scanio's modern spin on Creole cuisine.

10 Atchafalaya
MAP G6 ■ 901 Louisiana Ave ■ 504-891-9626 ■ $$$

The Bloody Mary bar (see p60) draws crowds to brunch. Dinner choices include shrimp and grits, and gumbo.

See map on pp72–3

🔟 CBD and Warehouse District

The hustle and bustle that surrounds daily activity in the downtown area extends all the way through the Warehouse and Central Business districts (CBD). Like that of any other major American city, New Orleans' downtown is a hub of commerce, entertainment, dining, and shopping. But what distinguishes this area is the large concentration of citizens who live here, as well as the number of historic 19th-century buildings that exist in between the profusion of newer structures. Today, many of the old warehouses in these neighborhoods have been converted into stylish spaces housing jazz bars, restaurants, hotels, galleries, and museums.

CBD AND WAREHOUSE DISTRICT

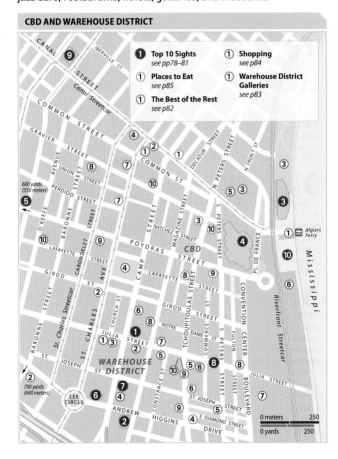

1 Top 10 Sights *see pp78–81*	**1** Shopping *see p84*
1 Places to Eat *see p85*	**1** Warehouse District Galleries *see p83*
1 The Best of the Rest *see p82*	

Canal Street, the main boulevard in New Orleans' downtown area

1 Canal Street

This historic road *(see pp36–7)* originally divided old New Orleans into the French and American parts. Named for a proposed canal that was never built, it is the most in-demand spot to watch the Mardi Gras parade, and is lined with restaurants, stores, and luxury hotels. The Canal streetcar is a good way to explore the sights along the length of this road.

2 The National World War II Museum

Housing a large collection of World War II memorabilia, this museum *(see pp18–19)* was created to honor all the Americans who contributed to the war effort. Take the "Behind the Lines Tour," a fascinating visit to the museum's vault with a curator.

3 Audubon Aquarium of the Americas

MAP N5 ■ 1 Canal St ■ 504-861-2537 ■ Open Apr–Aug: 10am–5pm daily; Sep–Mar: Tue–Sun (timings vary; check website) ■ Adm ■ www. audubonnatureinstitute.org

At the edge of the French Quarter, this aquarium is housed in an ultra-modern building on the banks of the Mississippi. It has undergone a major makeover and features three levels of displays of live creatures that inhabit the sea. From the entertaining penguin colony to the huge array of sharks and walk-through underwater tunnel, the aquarium appeals to visitors of all ages. On arrival, be sure to check out the timing of animal feedings for that day.

4 Harrah's New Orleans Casino

A block away from the Mississippi River, Harrah's *(see p36)* provides entertainment options ranging from gambling to fine dining. The casino has over 2,000 slot machines, and games such as roulette, baccarat, and poker on more than 100 tables. It also has the upscale Besh Steak House, the cocktail lounge Masquerade, a lavish buffet restaurant, and several smaller restaurants.

Harrah's New Orleans Casino

The sleek exterior of the Caesars Superdome

5 Caesars Superdome

MAP N1 ▪ 1500 Sugarbowl Drive ▪ 504-587-3663 ▪ Call for timings ▪ Adm ▪ www.mb superdome.com

This saucer-shaped landmark seating more than 70,000 people is home to the local football team, the Saints. However, the Caesars Superdome is much more than just a sports venue: it also hosts major conventions, exhibitions, car shows, and rock concerts.

Ogden Museum of Southern Art

6 Ogden Museum of Southern Art

MAP Q3 ▪ 925 Camp St ▪ 504-539-9650 ▪ Open 10am–5pm Wed–Mon, 10am–8pm Thu ▪ Adm ▪ www.ogden-museum.org

This multilevel building with an industrial feel houses the finest and most diverse collection of Southern art in the U.S. A substantial part of businessman Roger Ogden's huge collection was donated to create this museum, which features everything from folk art to contemporary pieces.

7 Contemporary Arts Center New Orleans

MAP Q3 ▪ 900 Camp St ▪ 504-528-3800 ▪ Open 11am–5pm Wed–Mon ▪ Adm ▪ www.cacno.org

Formed in 1976, the Contemporary Arts Center (CAC) was one of the earliest art addresses in the entire Warehouse District. The cavernous building has been refashioned into a workspace for artists, exhibitions, and theater. Although the focus is on visual arts, educational programs, and performing arts are highlights too.

8 Julia Street

MAP Q3

New Orleans' gallery neighborhood, this is one of the main streets in the Warehouse District, featuring some of the most appealing historic architecture. At the annual White Linen Night street party hosted here in August, people can browse through art, eat and drink, and enjoy live music.

CANAL STREET: THE FIRST NEUTRAL GROUND

With three traffic lanes, a streetcar, and a bus lane, Canal Street is one of the world's widest boulevards. The term "neutral ground" originated here in the 1800s, when Anglo-Americans took up residence in the city. The median strip became the place to settle disputes.

9 Saenger Theatre

The Italian Renaissance-style Saenger Theatre *(see p37)* stages a wide variety of shows, including concerts, Broadway musicals, and plays. Designed in the 1920s by noted New Orleans architect Emile Weil, the Saenger has an elegant mezzanine and towering arcade, while the main auditorium resembles the open-air courtyard of a 15th-century Italian villa, with archways and Greek and Roman statuary decorating the walls and a painted sky on the ceiling.

Exterior of the Saenger Theatre

10 Mississippi Riverfront

This stretch *(see pp22–3)* is popular for evening strolls, with public access through parks and walkways. The Spanish Plaza, with its large central fountain and colorful tiles, is a great place for visitors to relax and enjoy a view of the river.

Visitors by the fountain at Spanish Plaza

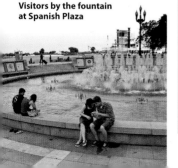

A WALK AROUND THE WAREHOUSE DISTRICT

▶ MORNING

Have a breakfast of shrimp and grits or crabmeat cheesecake at the **Palace Café** *(see p85)* on Canal Street, then make your way to the **Woldenberg Riverfront Park** *(see p22)*, a lovely green area with contemporary sculpture and a view of the river. Next to the park, to the south, is the **Audubon Aquarium of the Americas** *(see p79)*, which is fun to explore. Then walk a few blocks south to **Julia Street** to admire its quaint architecture and plethora of art galleries. Stop by the nationally acclaimed **Arthur Roger Gallery** *(see p83)*, the pinnacle of the local arts scene. Browse and shop at the street's many boutiques before making your way to **The National World War II Museum** *(see pp18–19)* to see its collection of war memorabilia. Afterward, take a break for a hearty Cajun-inspired lunch of fried alligator or chicken and andouille gumbo at **Cochon** *(see p85)*.

AFTERNOON

Walk back past The National World War II Museum to the **Ogden Museum of Southern Art** and the **Contemporary Arts Center New Orleans** for more visual stimuli and some fantastic pieces of art. End your day of culture at **Tommy's Cuisine** *(746 Tchoupitoulas St; 504-581-1103; closed Mon)*, with its Creole delicacies and great collection of wines. Later, make your way back to the Mississippi Riverfront to end your day with one of New Orleans' spectacular sunsets.

See map on p78 ←

The Best of the Rest

Algiers Ferry on the Mississippi

1 Algiers Ferry

MAP P5 ■ 6am–midnight ■ Adm from Algiers Point; free from Canal St

Visitors can take a ferry ride to experience the city from the river. This route starts from the foot of Canal Street and ends at the historic Algiers Point.

2 Southern Food & Beverage Museum

MAP R1 ■ 1504 Oretha C. Haley Blvd ■ 504-569-0405 ■ Open 11am–5:30pm Wed–Mon ■ Adm ■ www.natfab.org

Eating is a favored pastime in New Orleans, and this museum (see p45) hosts demonstrations, exhibits, lectures, and tastings of the South's food and drink.

3 Woldenberg Riverfront Park

The green area (see p22) along the banks of the Mississippi is perfect for biking, jogging, or just spending a lazy afternoon. It hosts festivals and events throughout the year.

4 Lafayette Square

MAP P3 ■ S. Maestri Pl

A green space hiding within the urban surrounds of the CBD, Lafayette Square is an oasis of tranquility. It also hosts a popular program of free summer concerts called Wednesdays at the Square.

5 The Howlin' Wolf

MAP Q4 ■ 907 S. Peters St ■ 504-522-9653

One of the few live music venues in the Warehouse District, The Howlin' Wolf (see p52) hosts rock, jazz, and blues concerts.

6 St. Patrick's Church

MAP P3 ■ 724 Camp St ■ 504-525-4413 ■ Timings vary ■ www.oldstpatricks.org

This Gothic-style church is a National Historic Landmark and an elegant reminder of old New Orleans.

7 Ernest N. Morial Convention Center

One of the largest convention centers (see p23) in the country, this building features state-of-the-art technology.

8 Mulate's Cajun Restaurant and Dance Hall

MAP Q4 ■ 201 Julia St ■ 504-522-1492

This restaurant is known for offering traditional Cajun food and lively Cajun music, plus dancing lessons for first timers. Do not miss the excellent crabmeat au gratin.

9 Preservation Resource Center

MAP Q4 ■ 923 Tchoupitoulas St ■ 504-581-7032 ■ Open 9am–5pm Mon–Fri ■ www.prcno.org

A nonprofit organization, this aims to preserve the historic neighborhoods and develop the resources of the city.

10 Loa

MAP N3 ■ 221 Camp St ■ 504-553-9550 ■ www.ihhotel.com

This shadowy, voodoo-themed bar in the International House Hotel (see p116) offers boutique wines and an array of cocktails.

Warehouse District Galleries

1 Sasik Gallery
MAP Q3 ▪ 541 Julia St
▪ 544-322-5055 ▪ Open 10am–5pm
Mon–Sat ▪ www.sasikart.com
Vibrant oil paintings by local artist
Beata Sasik adorn this gallery. It also
has beautifully crafted silver jewelry.

2 Callan Contemporary
MAP Q3 ▪ 518 Julia St ▪ 504-
525-0518 ▪ Open 10am–5pm Tue–Sat
▪ www.callancontemporary.com
Clean and minimalist, this gallery is
home to around 25 of the country's
most exciting artists.

3 Steve Martin Fine Art
MAP Q3 ▪ 624 Julia St ▪ 504-
566-1390 ▪ Open 10am–6pm daily
▪ www.stevemartinfineart.com
Internationally recognized, this gallery
displays works across various genres.

4 Contemporary Arts Center New Orleans
The CAC (see p80) is dedicated to
cutting-edge and even experimental
art. Both local and national artists
exhibit their works here.

5 Arthur Roger Gallery
MAP Q3 ▪ 432 & 434 Julia St
▪ 504-522-1999 ▪ Open 10am–
5pm Tue–Sat ▪ www.arthurroger
gallery.com
Established in 1978 by Arthur Roger,
a world-famous purveyor of fine art,
this gallery is one of the most high-
profile art spaces in the city.

Exhibition in the Arthur Roger Gallery

6 LeMieux Galleries
MAP Q4 ▪ 332 Julia St ▪ 504-
522-5988 ▪ Open 10am–5:30pm Mon–
Sat ▪ www.lemieuxgalleries.com
Artists from Louisiana and the
rest of the Gulf Coast are the focal
point of this contemporary gallery.

Contact Tracing, LeMieux Galleries

7 Octavia Art Gallery
MAP Q3 ▪ 454 Julia St ▪ 504-
309-4249 ▪ Open 10am–6pm Tue–Sat
▪ www.octaviaartgallery.com
This gallery displays the work of
both emerging and established
international contemporary artists.

8 New Orleans Glassworks
MAP P3 ▪ 727 Magazine St ▪ 504-529-
7279 ▪ Open 10am–5:30pm Mon–Sat
▪ www.neworleansglassworks.com
Around 250 artists showcase glass
art, sculpture, and printmaking here.

9 Soren Christensen Gallery
MAP Q4 ▪ 400 Julia St ▪ 504-569-9501
▪ Open 10am–5pm Tue–Sat ▪ www.
sorengallery.com
Photographs, sculptures, and
paintings focussing on Southern
art are displayed in a bright space.

10 Jonathan Ferrara Gallery
MAP Q4 ▪ 400A Julia St ▪ 504-
522-5471 ▪ Open 10am–5pm Mon–Sat
▪ www.jonathanferraragallery.com
This gallery has contemporary works
by regional and international artists.

See map on p78 ←

Shopping

(1) Meyer the Hatter
MAP N3 ■ 120 St. Charles Ave
■ 504-525-1048

This third-generation store features quality headwear for men in classic, contemporary, and trendy designs.

(2) Rubensteins
Owned by the same family since 1924, Rubensteins (see p37) is regarded as the finest men's clothing store in the city. It has also started stocking stylish womenswear.

(3) Shops at Canal Place
A luxury hotel, theaters, and a three-level shopping center with upscale retailers such as Saks Fifth Avenue and Brooks Brothers make up this complex (see p36).

(4) Adler's
MAP M3 ■ 722 Canal St
■ 504-523-5292

Considered one of the finest jewelry retailers in town, Adler's (see p62) is famous for its custom-designed pieces.

(5) Jack Sutton Fine Jewelry
MAP N4 ■ 365 Canal St
■ 504-522-8080

Elegant jewelry, including ready-to-wear designs as well as custom pieces, is on offer at this high-end store.

(6) The Outlet Collection at Riverwalk
This complex (see p23) houses shops, bars, galleries, restaurants, and other entertainment venues.

(7) Stella Jones Gallery
MAP N3 ■ 201 St. Charles Ave
■ 504-568-9050

This interesting exhibition space for African-American artists presents a diverse collection of works. Look out for talks and lectures.

(8) The Watch & Clock Shop
MAP N3 ■ 824 Gravier St
■ 504-525-3961

Specializing in antiques, this store is dedicated to stylish timepieces. Ask to see the upstairs showroom for the most exclusive items. The store also offers repairs.

(9) Friend
MAP P3 ■ 600 Carondelet St
■ 504-342-2162

Attached to the Ace Hotel, this hip menswear store is not the biggest around, but it has a substantial stock of clothing, accessories, and gifts.

(10) Southern Costume Company
MAP P3 ■ 951 Lafayette St ■ 504-523-4333

If you're visiting for Mardi Gras, head to this store selling inventive looks created by local costume designers. Rental options and bespoke costumes are also available.

The Outlet Collection at Riverwalk

Places to Eat

1 Palace Café
MAP N3 ■ 605 Canal St
■ 504-523-1661 ■ $$$

Palace Café serves seafood and Creole specialties. The white chocolate bread pudding is excellent.

PRICE CATEGORIES

For a three-course meal for one, with half a bottle of wine (or equivalent meal), taxes, and extra charges.

$ under $25 $$ $25–$50 $$$ over $50

Palace Café's elegant interior

2 Herbsaint
MAP P3 ■ 701 St. Charles Ave
■ 504-524-4114 ■ $$$ ■ Closed Sun

Southern classics such as Muscovy duck leg confit and dark roux gumbos (seafood stew flavored with a dark brown sauce) are the highlights here.

3 August
MAP R4 ■ 301 Tchoupitoulas St
■ 504-299-9777 ■ $$$

This seasonally focused restaurant (see p60) offers innovative modern French cuisine served in an elegant room by knowledgeable staff.

Colorful dish from August

4 Cochon
MAP R4 ■ 930 Tchoupitoulas St
■ 504-588-2123 ■ $$$ ■ Closed Sun

The menu in this warehouse-style restaurant is pork-focused, and meat lovers will love Cochon's take on Cajun dishes. The boucherie plate is perfect for sharing with friends.

5 Emeril's
MAP Q4 ■ 800 Tchoupitoulas St
■ 504-528-9393 ■ $$$

Named for its famous chef, Emeril Lagasse, this restaurant features a diverse menu including andouille-crusted drum, a flaky freshwater fish.

6 La Boca
MAP Q4 ■ 870 Tchoupitoulas St
■ 504-525-8205 ■ $$$ ■ Closed Sun

One of the best steakhouses in town, La Boca offers traditional Argentinian cuisine, plus a remarkable wine list.

7 Luke
MAP P3 ■ 333 St. Charles Ave
■ 504-378-2840 ■ $$$

Towering plates of oysters, mussels, and seafood are served at this European-style brasserie with a menu favoring Creole flavors.

8 Compère Lapin
MAP P4 ■ 535 Tchoupitoulas St
■ 504-599-2119 ■ $$$

With a menu as diverse as the city itself (see p60), chef Nina Compton serves seasonal dishes such as crispy dirty rice and roasted banana zeppole.

9 Poydras & Peters
MAP P4 ■ 300 Poydras St ■ 504-595-3305 ■ $$$

This place (see p59) has an intriguing menu that offers a combination of Southern and Vietnamese cuisines.

10 The Grill Room
MAP N3 ■ 300 Gravier St
■ 504-522-1994 ■ $$$

Modern Louisiana cuisine is on offer at this high-end dining room in the Windsor Court Hotel.

See map on p78

🔟 French Quarter

This historic district is the oldest part of the city and was built by Jean-Baptiste Le Moyne de Bienville in 1721. Also known as the Vieux Carré or "the Quarter" to locals, it is a mix of evocative Spanish- and French-influenced architecture, and features a lively nightlife and restaurant scene. The epicenter is Jackson Square, named for President Andrew Jackson and populated by local artists, musicians, and tarot-card readers. Bourbon Street cuts a lurid swathe through the center with its karaoke bars and strip clubs, while Royal Street provides a cultural contrast with its elegant galleries and antiques shops. Decatur Street runs parallel to the Mississippi River and is home to the bustling French Market, where traders have been active since 1791.

Busking on Royal Street

FRENCH QUARTER

Previous pages Balconies with flowers in the French Quarter

Neon-lit Bourbon Street, one of New Orleans' main entertainment hubs

1 Bourbon Street

A hotbed of shops, restaurants, clubs, and other entertainment options, Bourbon Street *(see pp32–3)* turns into a pedestrian zone at night, with visitors going from club to club, dancing, drinking, and partying. Liquor laws allow drinking on the streets, so all the bars serve drinks to go.

2 Old Ursuline Convent Museum

MAP L5 ■ 1100 Chartres St ■ 504-529-3040 ■ Tours: 10am–4pm Tue–Fri (last tour 3:15pm), 9am–3pm Sat (last tour 2:15pm) ■ Adm

Completed in 1752, the Old Ursuline Convent is the oldest surviving building in the Mississippi River Valley. Now a museum open for self-guided tours, the former convent was home to the founding Ursuline Sisters and has a beautiful hand-crafted cypress staircase, paintings, religious statuary, and bronze busts. The building has served as an orphanage, a hospital, and a residence hall for bishops.

3 Jackson Square

Originally used for meetings and public executions, Jackson Square *(see pp26–7)* is now a beautiful garden. It is adjacent to the St. Louis Cathedral *(see p90)* and the Pontalba Apartment Buildings *(see p27)*, which are the oldest apartments in the country. In the center of the square stands a statue of former U.S. president Andrew Jackson, dedicated to his victory at the Battle of New Orleans in 1815. Along the perimeter are restaurants and novelty shops, all facing out to the artists, fortune tellers, palm readers, and jazz musicians who spend their days working in the square.

ESPLANADE AVE

0 meters 200
0 yards 200

9

6

N PETERS STREET

Mississippi

4 The Historic New Orleans Collection

The history of New Orleans goes back centuries, and The Historic New Orleans Collection *(see pp20–21)* is the pre-eminent collection of archives on the city, and includes a permanent exhibit on French Quarter history. It began with the donation of a personal collection in 1966, but has since expanded into a state-of-the-art resource center on Louisiana. Today, it also serves as a facility for researchers.

A poster from The Historic New Orleans Collection

5 St. Louis Cathedral

MAP L4 ■ 615 Pere Antoine Alley ■ 504-525-9585 ■ Tours: 8:30am–4pm daily ■ www.stlouiscathedral.org

Dedicated to King Louis IX of France, St. Louis is the oldest continuously active Roman Catholic cathedral in the U.S. The original wooden church was built in 1718 but was consumed by a hurricane. A sturdier structure was erected in 1727 but was ruined again, this time in a fire. The church was then rebuilt in the mid-19th century. Its beautiful interior is maintained by the Archdiocese of New Orleans. Behind the church is a garden with an imposing statue of Jesus. In the evening spotlights illuminate the statue, projecting a giant shadow on the church's back wall, adding to its ambience.

6 The French Market and Lower Decatur Street

MAP L6 ■ 1009 N. Peters St ■ Open 8am–5pm Thu–Mon ■ www.frenchmarket.org

Located between Decatur Street and the Mississippi, the French Market is more than 200 years old. As well as a produce market, there is a flea market here. Lower Decatur Street is a mix of open yards and garages selling antiques and costume items, plus bars, music venues, and restaurants, as well as gift and T-shirt shops.

7 Jean Lafitte National Historical Park Visitor Center

MAP M4 ■ 419 Decatur St ■ 504-589-3882 ■ Open 9am–4:30pm Tue–Sat ■ www.nps.gov

A great place for a quick lesson on the geography, history, and culture of the Mississippi River Delta region, this park consists of six sites in Louisiana, all offering informative guided tours by park rangers.

8 Chartres Street

MAP M4

Even in the heart of the French Quarter, some streets offer welcome respite from the bustling crowds. Step from the sea of "to-go" cups on Bourbon Street and Royal Street onto Chartres Street (pronounced "charters"), which runs between

St. Louis Cathedral, facing Jackson Square

St. Louis Cathedral and Jackson Square. Browse antiques stores and galleries, sample classic New Orleans cuisine, and admire some of the finest architecture in the French Quarter.

Royal Street, popular with shoppers

9 Royal Street

This street offers exquisite antiques shops, fine jewelry stores, sophisticated cocktail bars, famous restaurants, and art galleries that attract collectors from all over the world (see pp28–31). It also features the grandest mansions in the French Quarter. Every afternoon, street musicians and performers entertain visitors.

10 New Orleans Jazz National Historical Park

MAP L5 ■ 916 N. Peters St ■ 504-589-4841 ■ Open 10am–4:30pm Tue–Sat ■ www.nps.gov

Located within Louis Armstrong Park, the New Orleans Jazz National Historical Park honors the city as the birthplace of jazz. The park is home to Perseverance Hall, a rare surviving original jazz dance hall built in 1819, where African-American musicians trained and performed for both white and African-American audiences.

HAUNTED HOTEL

Rumors of ghosts float about the Hotel Monteleone (see p29). Guests and staff have reported doors opening on their own, elevators stopping on the wrong floor, and ghostly images of children. It is on the list of most haunted hotels in the country.

A DAY IN THE FRENCH QUARTER

▶ MORNING

Start your day early and avoid the crowds at **Café du Monde** (see p58), where you can fuel up on café au lait and beignets. From there, walk a few blocks along to the **French Market**, where local farmers will be setting up their produce stalls – you can get first pick at the flea market, which has artworks, jewelry, and souvenirs. There's time to dip into the **New Orleans Jazz Museum** (see p92) at the Old U.S. Mint before walking back to **Central Grocery & Deli** (see p95), which has the most famous muffulettas in town. You'll need just a half, or you can split one while people-watching.

AFTERNOON

Head over to **Bourbon Street** (see p89) in the early evening and grab a Sazerac cocktail at the **Bourbon House Restaurant** (see p32), coupled with a dish or two from their famous oyster bar (the happy hour runs 4–6pm). This sets you up nicely for dinner at the historic and atmospheric **Arnaud's** (see p95), famous for its soufflé potatoes. Be sure to check out the Mardi Gras Museum upstairs. After dinner, wander over to **Chart Room** (see p94), a laid-back, small bar with an old-school juke box, for a beer. End the night with some traditional jazz at **Fritzel's European Jazz Pub** (see p94), where visitors squeeze in to enjoy some of New Orleans' finest music.

See map on pp88–9 ←

The Best of the Rest

1 Gallier House
James Gallier, Jr. was one of the most prominent 19th-century architects in New Orleans. His elegant Victorian home is now a museum *(see p29)* showcasing the architecture of the period.

2 Beauregard-Keyes House and Garden
MAP L5 ▪ 1113 Chartres St ▪ 504-523-7257 ▪ Open 10am–3pm Mon–Sat ▪ Adm ▪ www.bkhouse.org
Built in 1826, this house is named for Confederate general P. G. T. Beauregard and author Frances Parkinson Keyes. It features raised center-hall architecture.

3 New Orleans Pharmacy Museum
MAP M4 ▪ 514 Chartres St ▪ 504-565-8027 ▪ Open noon–5pm Wed–Sat ▪ Adm ▪ www.pharmacymuseum.org
The first licensed pharmacy in the U.S. is now a museum *(see p47)* containing old medicinal objects. The docents regale visitors with tales of medical history.

4 Lafitte's Blacksmith Shop Bar
Originally a late-18th-century tavern, Lafitte's Blacksmith Shop *(see p32)* is one of the oldest buildings in New Orleans. It is also one of the hottest bars in the city today.

Popular Lafitte's Blacksmith Shop Bar

5 Rodrigue Studio
George Rodrigue became famous for his humorous "Blue Dog" series *(see p29)*. His paintings are now serious collector's items.

6 Michalopoulos
MAP M4 ▪ 617 Bienville St ▪ 504-558-0505 ▪ Open 10am–6pm Mon–Wed (to 9pm Thu–Sun) ▪ www.michalopoulos.com
Colorful, contemporary works by celebrated New Orleans artist James Michalopoulos are displayed here.

7 Madame John's Legacy
MAP L5 ▪ 632 Dumaine St ▪ 504-568-6968 ▪ Closed for restoration; check website ▪ www.louisianastatemuseum.org
This 18th-century Creole mansion exemplifies French colonial architecture in North America.

8 Callan Fine Art
MAP N4 ▪ 240 Chartres St ▪ 504-524-0025 ▪ Call for timings ▪ www.callanfineart.com
This place holds European art from 1830 to 1950 covering the Academic Art style, the American Barbizon style, and modern works.

9 New Orleans Jazz Museum
MAP L6 ▪ 400 Esplanade Ave ▪ 504-568-6993 ▪ Open 10am–4:30pm Tue–Sun ▪ Adm ▪ www.nolajazzmuseum.org
The Old U.S. Mint now houses the New Orleans Jazz Museum *(see p45)*.

10 Galerie d'Art Français
MAP M4 ▪ 541 Royal St ▪ 504-581-6925 ▪ Call for timings ▪ www.neworleansfrenchart.com
A selection of 20th-century French art, including many Impressionist works, are housed here.

Shopping

Intimate Bourbon French Parfums

(1) Bourbon French Parfums
MAP L4 ■ 805 Royal St ■ 504-522-4480 ■ www.neworleansperfume.com
This tiny perfumery has been custom blending lovely fragrances since 1843.

(2) The Brass Monkey
MAP M4 ■ 407 Royal St ■ 504-561-0688
One of the French Quarter's most eclectic gift shops, the Brass Monkey features a large collection of Limoges figurines and miniature boxes.

Maskarade mask shop

(3) Jack Sutton Fine Jewelry
MAP M4 ■ 315 Royal St ■ 504-522-0555 ■ www.jacksutton.com
The city's premier fine jewelry destination offers everything from hip-hop jewelry to diamonds.

(4) Royal Antiques Ltd.
MAP M4 ■ 309 Royal St ■ 504-524-7033 ■ www.royalantiques.com
Known for its fine art and furnishings, Royal Antiques sells beautiful mirrors, clocks, and lamps.

(5) Fifi Mahony's
MAP L5 ■ 934 Royal St ■ 504-525-4343
In a town that loves fancy-dress costumes, Fifi Mahony's is the perfect store, stocking party wigs, cosmetics, and unique accessories.

(6) Moss Antiques
MAP M4 ■ 411 Royal St ■ 504-522-3981 ■ www.mossantiques.com
A family-owned antiques store, Moss Antiques sells art, china, furniture, and chandeliers, as well as a constantly evolving and diverse inventory of new acquisitions.

(7) Fleur de Paris
This popular European-style boutique (see p29) also offers fine hats, couture fashion, exquisite jewelry, lingerie, and a collection of elegant beaded handbags.

(8) Maskarade
MAP L4 ■ 630 St. Ann St ■ 504-568-1018 ■ www.themaskstore.com
New Orleanians love masks and this shop provides some wonderfully original ones. These are available to buy all year, not just during Mardi Gras.

(9) Faulkner House Books
This small, charming bookstore (see p27) is a real treat for book lovers. It specializes in rarities, first editions, and works by renowned American authors. It is also the home of the Pirate's Alley Faulkner Society, fostering the literary community of New Orleans for over 20 years.

(10) Erzulie's Voodoo Store
MAP L4 ■ 807 Royal St ■ 504-525-2055 ■ www.erzulies.com
Part retail store and part spiritual and psychic services center, this is a place with a whole lot of character.

See map on pp88–9

Nightlife

(1) Beachbum Berry's Latitude 29

MAP N4 ▪ 321 N Peters St ▪ 504-609-3811 ▪ www.latitude29nola.com

Jeff Berry is a global expert on the tiki cocktail, served here in kitschy yet beautiful drinkware.

(2) Oz

MAP L4 ▪ 800 Bourbon St ▪ 504-593-9491

Located in the gay district, Oz is the premier dance club in the area. There are live shows, and the music carries on late into the night.

Cocktail from French 75

(3) The Jazz Playhouse

Live jazz revues and tasteful burlesque performances take place nightly at this upscale jazz club (see pp32–3) tucked inside the Royal Sonesta Hotel.

(4) Cat's Meow Karaoke Club

This lively karaoke club (see p32) is a non-stop party, offering its guests playlists covering hundreds of songs.

(5) Fritzel's European Jazz Pub

MAP L4 ▪ 733 Bourbon St ▪ 504-586-4800

This (see p53) is one of the few places on Bourbon Street where you can hear traditional New Orleans jazz.

(6) Chart Room

MAP M4 ▪ 300 Chartres St ▪ 504-522-1708

A cozy, old-school neighborhood bar, Chart Room has cheap drinks and draws a raucous crowd of regulars and tourists alike.

(7) French 75

MAP M3 ▪ 813 Bienville St ▪ 504-523-5433

This small bar is welcoming and sophisticated. Order the signature French 75 cocktail (champagne, gin, and lemon) and soufflé potatoes.

(8) Famous Door

Since the 1930s, this raucous Bourbon Street club (see p32) has been providing live entertainment, as well as night-long dancing every day of the week.

(9) Pat O'Brien's

There's a fun atmosphere at this iconic, long-running bar (see p32). Guests can keep the tall glass of their "Hurricane" as a souvenir.

(10) House of Blues

MAP N4 ▪ 225 Decatur St ▪ 504-310-4999

From regional bands and solo acts to internationally acclaimed jazz, rock, and blues, the House of Blues (see p53) is the last word in live music.

A band performing at the legendary House of Blues

Places to Eat

PRICE CATEGORIES

For a three-course meal for one, with half a bottle of wine (or equivalent meal), taxes, and extra charges.

$ under $25 $$ $25–$50 $$$ over $50

1 Galatoire's Restaurant

The crown jewel of Bourbon Street, Galatoire's (see p32) is a historic spot dating back to 1905, and is one of the few restaurants left that require gentlemen to wear a jacket. It also has the liveliest Friday lunch in town.

2 Sylvain

MAP M4 ▪ 625 Chartres St ▪ 504-265-8123 ▪ $$$

Located in the French Quarter, Sylvain offers a fresh take on local dishes, paired with creative cocktails. There is also a lovely courtyard.

3 G. W. Fins

MAP M3 ▪ 808 Bienville St ▪ 504-581-3467 ▪ $$$

This seafood fine dining restaurant stands out for its distinctive dishes, such as halibut topped with thinly sliced scallops and served with lobster risotto.

4 Bayona

MAP M3 ▪ 430 Dauphine St ▪ 504-525-4455 ▪ $$$ ▪ Closed Sun

The flagship restaurant of chef Susan Spicer, this cottage has a lovely courtyard and a fine menu of creative Louisiana classics. Lunch is especially good value.

5 Bourbon House Restaurant

This restaurant (see p32) features an outstanding oyster bar and is renowned for its excellent Creole preparations, such as crabmeat-stuffed Gulf fish.

6 Brennan's

MAP M4 ▪ 417 Royal St ▪ 504-525-9711 ▪ $$$

Restored to its original 1940s glory, this iconic restaurant (see p59) serves classic dishes including turtle soup and redfish amandine.

7 Acme Oyster House

MAP M3 ▪ 724 Iberville St ▪ 504-522-5973 ▪ $$$

Enjoy hand-shucked Louisiana oysters, cold on the half shell, or chargrilled with garlic butter.

The bar area at Napoleon House

8 Napoleon House

MAP N4 ▪ 500 Chartres St ▪ 504-524-9752 ▪ $$

Locals and tourists line up for delicious po'boy sandwiches, popular muffulettas, and other Creole classics.

9 Arnaud's

MAP M3 ▪ 813 Bienville St ▪ 504-523-5433 ▪ $$$

An upscale place (see p60) offering Creole cuisine: try the spicy Shrimp Arnaud. After dinner, visit the Mardi Gras Museum on the second floor.

10 Central Grocery & Deli

MAP N4 ▪ 923 Decatur St ▪ 504-523-1620 ▪ $

This 1906 Italian store with just a few seats has the best muffulettas in town, which were invented right here.

See map on pp88–9

TOP10 Bywater, Marigny, and Treme

These downtown districts contain a wealth of food, nightlife, and entertainment options. The Marigny and Bywater districts, served by the Rampart-St. Claude streetcar, continue along the Mississippi's edge from the French Quarter. The Marigny is a leafy area with quirky cafés, musical Frenchmen Street, and a buzzing arts corridor. Hip Bywater is home to visual and performance arts venues, as well as to Crescent Park, while Treme is the oldest African-American neighborhood in the U.S. and has a proud musical and cultural heritage.

The Spotted Cat on Frenchmen Street

1 Frenchmen Street
MAP K6

The Frenchmen in question were leaders of an uprising against Spanish rule after Louisiana was ceded to Spain in 1768, and were executed for their trouble. The street is now the place to enjoy restaurants and a large number of live music clubs, ranging from traditional jazz to reggae to rock. Some of New Orleans' best clubs are here, including The Spotted Cat *(see p100)*. There is often live music in the street itself.

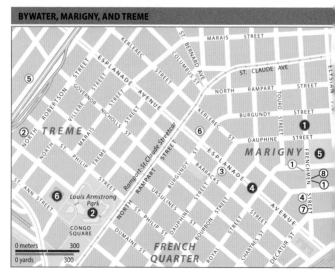

BYWATER, MARIGNY, AND TREME

2 Louis Armstrong Park and Congo Square
MAP K4 & L3 ■ 701 N. Rampart St

Right across the French Quarter, the lush Armstrong Park features a statue of New Orleans' favorite son, Louis "Satchmo" Armstrong, at the entrance. The site of jazz concerts and festivals throughout the year, the park is the start point for the Krewe of Barkus dog parade during Mardi Gras. At the southern end of the park lies Congo Square, an open space where enslaved workers and free "people of color" gathered to dance and sing throughout the 19th century, and where the seeds of jazz in the city were sown.

3 Piety Street Bridge
MAP N4 ■ Piety St at Chartres St

This huge, arching bridge at the entrance to Crescent Park (see p98) is constructed out of raw, untreated steel. The corrosive effects are in view, giving it the local nickname of "The Rusty Rainbow." It's a somewhat severe architectural statement, but a memorable one, paying homage to the railways that once ran here and to the industrial heritage of the area.

Colorful mansions along Esplanade Avenue

4 Esplanade Avenue
MAP K5

Separating the French Quarter from the Marigny, Esplanade Avenue stretches from the Mississippi River to New Orleans City Park. One of the most scenic streets in New Orleans, it is lined with lovely historical mansions dating back to the 19th century, when it was an important trade route and the address of choice for rich Creole citizens. There are also quaint bistros, cafés, traditional restaurants, and houses representing most of the architectural styles of the 18th and 19th centuries.

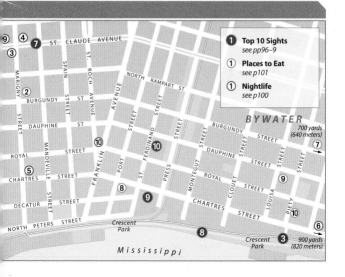

Top 10 Sights *see pp96–9*

Places to Eat *see p101*

Nightlife *see p100*

5 Washington Square
MAP K6

An urban park, Washington Square has green spaces lined with benches under old oak trees and is a good spot for throwing a frisbee or enjoying ball games. Many special events and festivals, including the annual Gay Pride Festival take place here.

6 Mahalia Jackson Theater for the Performing Arts
MAP K3 ▪ 1419 Basin St ▪ 504-525-1052 ▪ Call for timings ▪ Adm ▪ www.mahaliajacksontheater.com

Named for the acclaimed Queen of Gospel music, Mahalia Jackson, this world-class theater showcases Broadway musicals and diverse performances by famous musicians, comedians, dancers, ballet companies, and more. The highlight of Basin Street, this grand arena can seat 2,243 people.

The Mahalia Jackson Theater

7 St. Claude Avenue
MAP K4

The streetcar extension project is the cherry on the cake for the development of the St. Claude corridor. Well-established arts venues such as The AllWays Lounge and Theatre, Carnaval Lounge, and Hi-Ho Lounge *(see p100)* have been complemented by new restaurants, most of which serve dishes that fall outside of the usual Creole offerings. A fringe theater, The Theater at St. Claude, and a high-end food court, St. Roch Market, mean that more and more visitors are now exploring this lively and deserving area.

The stunning Crescent Park

8 Crescent Park

A 1.4-mile (2.2-km), 8-hectare (20-acre) green space that runs between Elysian Fields in the Marigny and Mazant Street in the Bywater, Crescent Park *(see p48)* has long stretches of grass and quiet paths, plus the remnants of an old wharf building. There are spots to sit next to the Mississippi. Thanks to the river's peculiar bends, in some places there are splendid views of the city skyline.

9 New Orleans Center for Creative Arts (NOCCA)
MAP N4 ▪ 2800 Chartres St ▪ 504-940-2787 ▪ www.nocca.com

Billed as "Louisiana's Arts Conservatory," NOCCA was established to train the city's young talent. Its major disciplines are dance, music, theater, and visual arts, but culinary and cinematic courses are also available. Famous graduates include Harry Connick, Jr., Terence Blanchard, and Wendell Pierce. The facility arranges

---

STREETCAR SCENE

A Rampart-St. Claude streetcar line runs from the Union Passenger Terminal on Calliope Street to Elysian Fields Avenue along the Treme and Marigny neighborhoods, and terminates near a cluster of bars and live music venues on St. Claude Avenue.

occasional student productions, usually around the end of term, which are sometimes open to the public (check online).

⑩ Marigny Opera House
725 St. Ferdinand St ■ 504-948-9998 ■ www.marignyoperahouse.org

Many New Orleans venues are former churches, but none is as impressive as this self-proclaimed "church of the arts." The building itself dates back to 1853. In 2011 it was transformed into a venue for classical music, dance, and theater. The Opera House has a strong line in operatic productions and contemporary dance.

Facade of Marigny Opera House

EXPLORING AROUND THE NEIGHBORHOODS

▶ MORNING

Start the day with a coffee at **Treme Coffeehouse** (1501 St. Philip St), just across from **Louis Armstrong Park**, then go for a stroll around the landscaped gardens, taking in **Congo Square** (see p97) and paying your respects to the statue of Louis Armstrong. As you exit, head toward the Marigny and walk through the colorful streets to riverside **Crescent Park**, where you can take photos of the New Orleans city skyline. From here, cross the **Piety Street Bridge** (see p97) back to the Bywater – lunch can be a few slices of pizza and a cold local beer at **Pizza Delicious** (see p101). **Euclid Records** (3301 Chartres St) and **Dr. Bob's Folk Art** (3027 Chartres St) are in the vicinity for some post-lunch music and art browsing.

AFTERNOON

Take a late afternoon walk to **Frenchmen Street** (see p96), with a stop at **The Spotted Cat Music Club** (see p100) for a cocktail and traditional jazz, or sample some small plates at **Three Muses** (see p101), where diners are entertained by local musicians. There is also the chance to see some of the city's best artists and impressive crafts at the nighttime-only **Frenchmen Art Market** (see p100) before continuing to St. Claude Avenue. From here, you'll have a choice of entertainment options – perhaps a DJ set at **Hi-Ho Lounge**, a burlesque show at The **AllWays Lounge and Theatre**, or a rock band at **Carnaval Lounge** (see p100), where – if you're still hungry – there's a great kitchen serving Mexican street food late into the night.

See map on pp96–7

Nightlife

Palace Art Market, a night-time event where visitors can buy local art

① Palace Art Market
MAP K6 ▪ 619 Frenchmen St
▪ 504-358-8287
Grab a cocktail from The Spotted Cat and wander around this night-time market, which sells paintings, sculpture, clothing, and souvenirs.

② Candlelight Lounge
MAP L2 ▪ 925 N. Robertson St
▪ 504-906-5877
The best brass bands in the city, including the Treme Brass Band themselves, play at this unassuming but colorful Treme venue (see p52).

③ The AllWays Lounge and Theatre
MAP K4 ▪ 2240 St. Claude Ave
▪ 504-218-5778
Every night has a different vibe at this kitsch venue (see p51), from comedy, drag, and burlesque, to folk music.

④ Hi-Ho Lounge
MAP K4 ▪ 2239 St. Claude Ave
▪ 504-945-4446
This place has inexpensive bar food and an eclectic mix of events, such as comedy, DJs, and some of the city's most risqué burlesque shows.

⑤ The Friendly Bar
MAP K6 ▪ 2301 Chartres St
▪ 504-943-8929
A laid-back neighborhood LGBTQ+ bar (see p55) that lives up to its name; serves great drinks.

⑥ Bacchanal
600 Poland Ave ▪ 504-948-9111
This well-stocked wine bar with a huge patio offers live music, plus hot food and cheese plates.

⑦ The Maison
MAP K6 ▪ 508 Frenchmen St
▪ 504-371-5543
The Maison (see p53) has a respectable menu for laid-back, early evening dinner jazz shows and three music stages for livelier late-night sets.

⑧ The Spotted Cat Music Club
MAP K6 ▪ 623 Frenchmen St
▪ 504-943-3887
Traditional jazz and swing dancing rule at The Spotted Cat, a lively Frenchmen institution that has a packed bar.

⑨ Carnaval Lounge
MAP K4 ▪ 2227 St. Claude Ave
▪ 504-265-8855
For those who are after punk, hip-hop, or other non-jazzy New Orleans music, this indie music bar (see p52) hits the spot.

⑩ Big Daddy's
MAP L4 ▪ 2513 Royal St
▪ 504-948-6288
With pool tables and a great selection of beers, always welcoming Big Daddy's (see p54) is a popular LGBTQ+ hangout in Treme.

Places to Eat

1 Three Muses
MAP K6 ■ 536 Frenchmen St
■ 504-252-4801 ■ $$

Part music venue, part restaurant,
Three Muses (see p53) fills up quickly.
Tasty small plates complement the
light jazz, while the cocktail list is
among the best downtown.

2 The Elysian Bar
MAP F3 ■ 2317 Burgundy St
■ 504-356-6769 ■ $$

Enjoy Southern-French cuisine at
the cozy bar or courtyard of this
elegant restaurant.

3 Port of Call
MAP J2 ■ 838 Esplanade Ave
■ 504-523-0120 ■ $$

The enduring popularity of this
burger joint (see p61) can be seen
in the lines out of the door.

4 Marigny Brasserie
MAP K6 ■ 640 Frenchmen St
■ 504-945-4472 ■ $$$

This chic and bright restaurant
has a seasonal menu where dishes
feature fresh, local ingredients.

Outdoor seating at Marigny

5 Ray's on the Ave
MAP J2 ■ 1031 N Claiborne
Ave ■ $

This hole-in-the-wall is a great place
for an after hours bowl of seafood
gumbo or a Creole sharing platter.

PRICE CATEGORIES

For a three-course meal for one, with half
a bottle of wine (or equivalent meal),
taxes, and extra charges.

$ under $25 $$ $25–$50 $$$ over $50

---

6 Buffa's
MAP J2 ■ 1001 Esplanade Ave
■ 504-949-0038 ■ $$

Comfort pub food, including burgers,
chicken wings, and chorizo bean
chilli, feature on the menu at this
late-night restaurant. There's regular
live rock and jazz music.

7 Sneaky Pickle
MAP M3 ■ 3200 Burgundy St
■ 504-218-5651 ■ $

Good-value nutritious and playful
vegan and vegetarian food is the
name of the game here, although
the occasional meat dish sneakily
makes the cut. The daily specials
are usually wonderful.

8 Small Mart
MAP L5 ■ 2700 Chartres St
■ 504-766-8740 ■ $

This café may be small, but it
wins over customers with a big
menu offering vegetarian and
vegan fare, with a focus on
samosas, bagels, and tofu plates.

9 Satsuma Café
3218 Dauphine St ■ 504-304-
5962 ■ $

For a breakfast and lunch comprised
of local organic ingredients, dine at
this community-driven café (see p59).
Do not miss the fresh-pressed juices
and leafy greens.

10 Pizza Delicious
617 Piety St ■ 504-676-8482
■ Closed Mon ■ $$

Routinely voted the best pizzeria
in the city, this busy place offers
a small but adventurous pizza
menu. It is complemented by a
very good line in pastas, salads,
and sides.

See map on pp96–7 ←

🔟 Mid-City

Extending from the French Quarter toward Lake Pontchartrain, Mid-City was carved out of a former plantation and is the greenest part of New Orleans. Dominated by the New Orleans City Park and intersected by the major thoroughfares of Canal Street and Esplanade Avenue, Mid-City is a predominantly residential area and is home to the original New Orleans families. Their distinct culture is exemplified by the fact that they have had their own Mardi Gras krewes since 1933. The Canal streetcar winds its way through this lovely neighborhood, which is dotted with cemeteries, canals, parkways, and Creole mansions. Although the area was heavily damaged by Hurricane Katrina, extensive reconstruction work has helped restore much of its delightful original charm.

The bright-red Canal streetcar

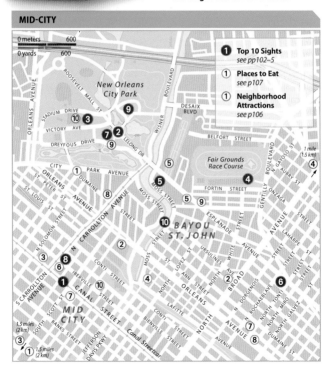

MID-CITY

0 meters 600
0 yards 600

New Orleans City Park

1 **Top 10 Sights**
see pp102–5

1 **Places to Eat**
see p107

1 **Neighborhood Attractions**
see p106

Fair Grounds Race Course

BAYOU ST. JOHN

MID CITY

Canal Streetcar

Colorful flowerbeds in bloom at the New Orleans Botanical Garden

1 Canal Streetcar
504-248-3900 ■ Adm
■ www.norta.com

This streetcar line, which begins at the Mississippi River, dates back to the mid-19th century. It travels through the CBD and well into Mid-City before coming to a stop at NOMA (see pp12–15). The vintage vehicles are fitted with wooden seats and painted a bright red. Locals use the streetcar as an inexpensive way to commute, whereas visitors find it the best mode of sightseeing, as the streetcar stops at most of the signiicant sights in Mid-City and travels at a leisurely pace.

2 New Orleans Museum of Art

An architectural and cultural gem in the Mid-City area, the New Orleans Museum of Art (NOMA) (see pp12–15) showcases ten permanent collections from all over the world, as well as high-profile rotating exhibitions. NOMA also has an active schedule of educational programs, children's programs, and special events that are open to the public. The museum gift shop offers some high-end and unique works of art, jewelry, accessories, and books.

Sculpture at the New Orleans Museum of Art

3 New Orleans Botanical Garden

Originally known as the City Park Rose Garden, these gardens (see p16) combine landscaping techniques with art and architecture. Today, more than 2,000 plant varieties can be found here. Mostly cared for by local volunteers, the gardens feature plants and flowers indigenous to Louisiana. Because of the tropical climate in New Orleans, the Botanical Garden showcases its best foliage and flowering plants almost year-round. The adjacent conservatory features a simulated tropical rain forest and a raging waterfall.

4 Fair Grounds Race Course & Slots
MAP D1 ■ 1751 Gentilly Blvd
■ 504-944-5515 ■ Adm for clubhouse
■ www.fairgroundsracecourse.com

Founded in 1852, the Fair Grounds are home to the third-oldest continuously running race track in the country as well as over 600 slot machines. The annual races are held from Thanksgiving Day to the end of March. Visitors can watch the races outdoors, or enjoy the comforts of the clubhouse, with fine dining and monitors to keep abreast of events at the track. The New Orleans Jazz and Heritage Festival (see p67) is held here.

A room in the Pitot House Museum

5 Pitot House Museum

MAP J3 ■ 1440 Moss St ■ 504-482-0312 ■ Tours 10am–3pm Wed–Sat ■ Adm ■ www.louisianalandmarks.org

Built in the late 18th century, Pitot House is a Creole colonial-style building on the banks of the Bayou St. John. It has had several owners, including lawyers and nuns, but is named for James Pitot, the first American mayor of New Orleans, who lived here from 1810 to 1819. It was beautifully restored by the Louisiana Landmarks Society in the 1960s, and is now a museum and a National Trust for Historic Preservation Partner Place. Organized tours are offered in the museum and its sprawling, elegant gardens.

VOODOO ON BAYOU ST. JOHN

Voodoo queen Marie Laveau *(see p41)* is famous for practicing her rituals on the banks of Bayou St. John. These ceremonies often involved ritualistic dances and animal sacrifices, and were witnessed by hundreds of people, believers and skeptics alike.

---

6 Degas House

MAP E2 ■ 2306 Esplanade Ave ■ 504-821-5009 ■ Tours by appt ■ Adm ■ www.degashouse.com

Edgar Degas, the renowned French Impressionist painter, lived in this house in 1872–3, and created at least 22 works of art during this period. Today, the house is one of the finest bed-and-breakfast inns in the city. There is an Edgar Degas House Tour, which explores the life of the artist during the Reconstruction Era (the period after the Civil War).

7 The Sydney and Walda Besthoff Sculpture Garden

Named after prominent art patrons collectors, the Besthoffs, this garden includes a collection of contemporary sculpture from across the world. The pieces, donated by the Besthoff Foundation, are displayed among the ancient oaks, magnolias, and tranquil lagoons in this exquisite garden, which is adjacent to the New Orleans Museum of Art *(see pp12–15)*. Free scavenger hunts around the garden are available.

8 Angelo Brocato's Ice Cream and Confectionery

MAP C2 ■ 214 N. Carrollton Ave ■ 504-486-0078

Angelo Brocato's has managed to retain its quality since opening in 1905. This charming old-world shop, run by the third generation of Brocatos, continues to attract the masses with Italian specialties such as *gelato* (low-fat ice cream), *spumoni* (molded Italian ice cream), *biscotti* (biscuits), and *torrone* (Italian nougat).

9 New Orleans City Park

Spanning 1,300 acres (526 ha), New Orleans City Park *(see pp16–17)* is one of the largest urban parks in the U.S., with a variety of gardens, sculptures, and buildings. Attractions such as Storyland and the Carousel Gardens Amusement Park *(see p17)* make this a great spot for kids. For visitors interested in outdoor activities, there are golf courses, tennis courts, and waterways for canoeing. The city park also includes the New Orleans Botanical Garden and hosts concerts, festivals, holiday light spectaculars, fundraisers, weddings, and other private events.

Vintage ride in New Orleans City Park

10 Bayou St. John
MAP J2

One of the most picturesque parts of Mid-City is Bayou St. John, an inner-city creek that separates two residential neighborhoods. Visitors can explore the area on foot or on a bicycle. The bayou is famous for having been the site of voodoo rituals in the 19th century.

Leafy area around Bayou St. John

A TOUR OF NEW ORLEANS CITY PARK

MORNING

Hop on to the Canal streetcar from the French Quarter or downtown area for a scenic ride into Mid-City. The last stop is the **New Orleans Museum of Art** *(see pp12–15)*, where you can get off and explore the museum, as well as walk along handsomely sculptured lawns and flower gardens, under centuries-old oaks, at the **New Orleans City Park** *(see pp16–17)*. This will work up an appetite, so treat yourself to a lavish meal at **Ralph's on the Park** *(see p107)*, which is famous for innovative Creole food as well as its fabulous location.

AFTERNOON

After lunch, walk around the beautifully designed **Sydney and Walda Besthoff Sculpture Garden**. Then make your way to the **New Orleans Botanical Garden** *(see p16)*, where you can view the **Louisiana Children's Museum** *(see p16)*, the miniature **Train Garden** *(see p17)* and enjoy a walk through the adjacent conservatory and theme gardens. Along the way, be sure to make a stop at **Storyland** *(see p17)*, a delightful place for people of all ages and a special treat for children. From here, walk over to the nearby **Carousel Gardens Amusement Park** *(see p17)*, which houses one of the few remaining antique wooden carousels in the country. Stop by **NOLA City Bark**, New Orleans' first officially designated dog park. End the day with a delicious *gelato* in one of the many flavors at **Angelo Brocato's Ice Cream and Confectionery**.

See map on p102 ⟵

Neighborhood Attractions

1 Mid-City Art Market
MAP B3 ▪ Carrollton Ave ▪ Open 10am–4pm

On the last Saturday of each month, local artists and craftsmen display and sell their wares at this market in Palmer Park.

A shotgun-style cottage

2 American Can Apartments
MAP H3 ▪ 3700 Orleans Ave ▪ 504-207-0090 ▪ www.americanneworleans.com

This condominium complex, a former manufacturing plant, is a prestigious Mid-City address with restaurants and a fashionable shopping area.

3 Rock 'n' Bowl
MAP B3 ▪ 3000 S. Carrollton Ave ▪ 504-861-1700

The atmosphere here (see p53) is happening, with live bands and other entertainment. If you enjoy a spot of bowling or love to party till the wee hours, this is where you should head.

4 Dillard University
2601 Gentilly Blvd ▪ 504-283-8822 ▪ www.dillard.edu

Established in 1869, this liberal-arts college was founded to educate newly freed enslaved workers. It offers majors in six academic fields.

5 St. Louis Cemetery No. 3
MAP D2 ▪ 3421 Esplanade Ave

A lesser-known cemetery, this is a peaceful place to see New Orleans' peculiar tombs close up. Marble and stone monuments are aplenty.

Angel at St. Louis Cemetery No. 3

6 Shotgun-Style Cottages
These narrow houses found throughout Mid-City have rooms lined up in a single row from front to back. The name derives from the fact that if a shotgun was fired, the bullet would pass straight through the house.

7 Willie Mae's Scotch House
MAP E2 ▪ 2401 St. Ann St ▪ 504-822-9503 ▪ Open 10am–8pm Mon–Sat

Said to serve the best fried chicken in New Orleans, Willie Mae's Scotch House has been very popular since it opened in 1957.

8 Pandora's Snowballs
MAP H3 ▪ 901 N. Carrollton Ave

A popular local hangout, this small corner shop offers cups of shaved ice in a variety of flavors, creamy soft-serve ice creams, and burgers.

9 Dueling Oaks
MAP H2 ▪ City Park

In the 19th century, this area in City Park served as a backdrop for countless duels. There's only one large overhanging tree left these days.

10 The Train Garden
A miniature replica of the city of New Orleans inside the Botanical Garden (see p16), this garden (see p17) has a fully operating train and buildings made out of natural materials.

Places to Eat

1 Ralph's on the Park
MAP G2 ▪ 900 City Park Ave
▪ 504-488-1000 ▪ $$$

This stellar restaurant, run by Ralph Brennan, features globally inspired Creole cuisine. The pork schnitzel and the crab pasta with gremolata are particularly recommended.

2 Crescent City Steaks
MAP D2 ▪ 1001 N. Broad St
▪ 504- 821-3271 ▪ Closed Mon ▪ $$$

The steaks at this dining room, a favorite since 1934, are outstanding. Curtains wrap around private booths.

3 Café Minh
MAP C2 ▪ 4139 Canal St
▪ 504-482-6266 ▪ Closed Sun ▪ $$

Renowned for its French-Vietnamese fusion cuisine, Café Minh's specials include coconut shrimp, crab cakes, and crabmeat and sweet corn soup.

4 Parkway Bakery and Tavern
MAP D2 ▪ 538 Hagan Ave ▪ 504-482-3047 ▪ Closed Tue ▪ $

This quaint shop serves some of the best fried shrimp po'boys (see p57) and roast beef sandwiches in the city.

5 Lola's
MAP D2 ▪ 3312 Esplanade Ave
▪ 504-488-6946 ▪ $$$

This popular Spanish restaurant allows patrons to bring their own wine. Try the seafood paella.

6 Venezia
MAP C2 ▪ 134 N. Carrollton Ave ▪ 504-488-7991 ▪ Closed Mon & Tue ▪ $$

Thanks to its traditional Italian dishes, Venezia is a popular local haunt. The pizzas are excellent.

7 Mandina's Restaurant
MAP C2 ▪ 3800 Canal St ▪ 504-482-9179 ▪ $$

A local institution, Mandina's serves delicacies such as jambalaya and a hearty gumbo (see p56).

PRICE CATEGORIES

For a three-course meal for one, with half a bottle of wine (or equivalent meal), taxes, and extra charges.

$ under $25 $$ $25–$50 $$$ over $50

8 Dooky Chase
MAP E3 ▪ 2301 Orleans Ave ▪ 504-821-0600 ▪ Closed Sat–Mon ▪ $$$

Run by legendary chef Leah Chase, famous for her "Creole Soul" food, Dooky Chase (see p61) has delicious home cooking.

9 Café Degas
MAP D2 ▪ 3127 Esplanade Ave ▪ 504-945-5635 ▪ Closed Mon & Tue ▪ $$

Named for the Impressionist artist Edgar Degas, this pretty French bistro (see p59) has light, subtle dishes.

Charming ambience at Café Degas

10 Liuzza's
MAP C2 ▪ 3636 Bienville St ▪ 504-482-9120 ▪ Closed Mon ▪ $$

Famous for its meatballs, seafood lasagna, jambalaya, and huge, icy "fishbowls" of draft beer, Liuzza's is a busy but friendly neighborhood diner.

See map on p102 ←

Streetsmart

Bright-red streetcars, commonly
seen on the streets of New Orleans

Getting Around

Arriving by Air

Located about 15 miles (24 km) from downtown New Orleans, the **Louis Armstrong International Airport** is the city's main airport. It serves all the major U.S. airlines.

Public transport options from the airport include the no. 202 Airport Express run by **RTA** (Regional Transport Authority), with nine daily trips priced at $1.50; an inexpensive shared shuttle bus operated by **Airport Shuttle New Orleans**, for downtown hotels; and cabs, which you can find at the stand outside the arrivals hall. A typical trip downtown by taxi costs $35–40.

Domestic Train Travel

Three major **Amtrak** trains serve the city: City of New Orleans, from Chicago; Crescent, from New York's Penn Station; and Sunset Limited, from Orlando and Los Angeles. All trains arrive at New Orleans Union Passenger Terminal, located at 1001 Loyola Avenue at the edge of the CBD.

Long-Distance Bus Travel

Modern long-distance buses operated by **Greyhound Bus Lines** serve New Orleans from around 4,000 U.S. locations and arrive at New Orleans Union Passenger Terminal, which is shared with Amtrak rail services.

Public Transportation

The RTA is New Orleans' main public transport authority and runs the city's buses and streetcar services. Safety and hygiene measures, time-tables, ticket information, and transport maps can be obtained from the RTA website. The RTA's GoMobile app provides live transport information.

Tickets

The standard fare for a single journey on the bus or streetcar is $1.25. Transfers cost 25 cents each. A one-day pass is $3. Single journeys and one-day passes can be purchased directly from the bus driver or a streetcar operator, with cash only. An RTA Jazzy Pass, available for 1-, 3-, and 31-day periods, lets you ride both buses and streetcars. These passes can be purchased online from the RTA website and GoMobile app, or from various vendors across New Orleans, such as the ticket machines (cash only) along the Canal Streetcar line.

Buses

Bus stops are indicated by white and yellow signs displaying the RTA logo. The route numbers of the buses stopping there are usually listed at the bottom of the sign. Buses stop only at designated bus stops, which are located every two or three blocks, depending on the area of the city. On boarding the bus, put the exact change or number of tokens in the fare box, or show your Jazzy Pass to the driver. Smoking, drinking, eating, and playing music are all prohibited on buses.

Streetcars

New Orleans' five street-car lines make a pleasant, leisurely way to get around the city, stopping frequently at major sights. No visitor should miss the opportunity to travel on the oldest streetcar in the U.S., St. Charles Streetcar (p73).

Ferries and Steamboats

New Orleans Ferry services run from the CBD to New Orleans' West Bank neighborhood. The Chalmette ferry accommodates cars, while the Algiers service is only for foot passengers.The journey takes only a few minutes and affords great views looking back over the New Orleans skyline.

Paddlewheel steam-boats offer Mississippi dinner cruises and after-noon tours. Book these via the **New Orleans Steamboat Company** or **Creole Queen**.

Taxis

The city's taxis are inexpensive, convenient, and highly recommended for trips after dark to areas outside the French Quarter. Cabs are easily found at airports, bus and train stations, all major hotels, and taxi stands. For time-sensitive journeys, pre-book a taxi with **United Cabs** or another company. All fares are metered according to the distance traveled.

Car Rental

Rental car companies are located at the airport and other locations in the city. To rent a car in the U.S. you must be at least 25 years old with a valid driving license and a clean record. Agencies require a major credit card. Damage and liability insurance is recommended.

Driving

The good public transportation network and short distances between sights make driving in central New Orleans unnecessary, but a car is convenient if you wish to visit the surrounding countryside, or the nearby Louisiana cities of Baton Rouge and Lafayette.

In central New Orleans, be prepared for heavy traffic and a severe shortage of parking facilities, especially in the French Quarter.

New Orleans is notorious for large potholes; drive carefully and make sure there is paved road ahead. Frequent heavy downpours can cause street flooding. Make sure to drive slowly through standing water, or find another route.

Rules of the Road

Traffic drives on the right-hand side of the road, and the speed limit is generally 35 mph (56 km/h) unless otherwise stated. When it is safe to do so you may turn right on a red light.

If a school bus stops to let passengers off, all traffic from both sides must stop and wait for the bus to drive off.

Cycling

Cycling in New Orleans is easy thanks to the city's flat, gridded network of streets, and bike-friendly initiatives. All city buses are equipped with bike racks, allowing you to combine modes of transport. Be sure to lock your bike securely when you park it, as bicycle thefts are common. **Bicycle Michael's** and **FreeWheelin' Bike Tours** offer rental services, as well as guided tours. The city's bike sharing scheme, **Blue Bikes**, has stations around the city. It can be used by registering online and then paying with a credit card.

The Lafitte Greenway (p46) is a 3-mile-(5-km-) long pedestrian and cycle trail linking Armstrong Park to City Park.

Walking

New Orleans is a great city to explore on foot. Walking allows you to take in the architecture and the details of the historic buildings. The downtown areas are close enough to walk between, and from the CBD all the way to the Bywater is only a couple of miles' walk through pleasant surroundings. Wear comfortable shoes; some sidewalks and streets are very old and uneven. Take care also when walking around at night. It is best to stick to the busiest streets and avoid poorly lit areas.

DIRECTORY

ARRIVING BY AIR

Airport Shuttle New Orleans
🌐 airportshuttle neworleans.com

Louis Armstrong International Airport
🌐 flymsy.com

RTA
🌐 norta.com

DOMESTIC TRAIN TRAVEL

Amtrak
🌐 amtrak.com

LONG-DISTANCE BUS TRAVEL

Greyhound Bus Lines
🌐 greyhound.com

FERRIES AND STEAMBOATS

Creole Queen
🌐 creolequeen.com

New Orleans Ferry
🌐 norta.com

New Orleans Steamboat Company
🌐 neworleanssteam boatcompany.com

TAXIS

United Cabs
🌐 unitedcabs.com

CYCLING

Bicycle Michael's
🌐 bicyclemichaels.co

Blue Bikes
🌐 bluebikesnola.com

FreeWheelin' Bike Tours
🌐 neworleans biketour.com

Practical Information

Passports and Visas

For entry requirements, including visas, consult your nearest U.S. embassy or check the **U.S. Department of State** website. Canadian and Mexican visitors require a valid passport to enter the U.S. Citizens of Australia, New Zealand, the UK, and the EU do not need a visa, but must apply in advance for an Electronic System for Travel Authorization (**ESTA**) visa waiver and have a valid passport. All other visitors will need a passport and tourist visa to enter.

Government Advice

Now more than ever, it is important to consult both your and the U.S. government's advice before traveling. The **UK Foreign and Commonwealth Office**, the U.S. Department of State, and the **Australian Department of Foreign Affairs and Trade** offer the latest information on security, health, and local regulations.

Customs Information

You can find information on the laws relating to goods and currency taken in or out of the U.S. on the **U.S. Customs and Border Protection Agency** website.

Insurance

We recommend that you take out a comprehensive insurance policy, covering theft, loss of belongings, medical care, cancellations, and delays, and read the small print carefully. There is no universal healthcare in the U.S. for citizens or visitors and healthcare is very expensive so it is particularly important to take out comprehensive medical insurance.

Health

The U.S. has a world-class healthcare system. However, costs for medical and dental care can quickly escalate. You will be asked to pay in advance. Keep all receipts to make a claim on your insurance later.

There are plenty of walk-in medical clinics and emergency rooms throughout New Orleans. **CrescentCare** offers convenient walk-in or by-appointment services at locations around the city. For urgent medical care, head to the emergency room at either of the city's main hospitals – **Touro Infirmary** or the **University Medical Center New Orleans** (UMCNO). For dental emergencies, call UMCNO or the **New Orleans Dental Association**.

Pharmacies are often an excellent source of advice. They can diagnose minor ailments and suggest appropriate treatment. The main pharmacy chains in New Orleans are **RiteAid** and **Walgreens**. There are several 24-hour pharmacies near the French Quarter.

Unless otherwise stated, tap water in New Orleans and the state of Louisiana is safe to drink.

No inoculations are required to visit the U.S. For information regarding COVID-19 vaccination requirements, consult government advice.

Smoking, Drugs, and Alcohol

Smoking is prohibited in all public buildings, bars, restaurants, and stores in New Orleans. Cigarettes can be purchased by those over the age of 18; proof of age will be required.

The legal minimum age for drinking alcohol is 21, and even those who look obviously older will need photo ID as proof of age in order to purchase alcohol and be allowed into bars. In New Orleans it is legal to drink alcohol in public (in a can or plastic container) but it is illegal to carry an open container of alcohol in your car, and penalties for driving under the influence of alcohol are severe. Louisiana strictly enforces its drink-drive limit of 0.08 per cent BAC (blood alcohol content).

Possession of illegal drugs is prohibited and could result in a hefty prison sentence.

ID

It is not compulsory to carry ID at all times in New Orleans. If you are asked by police to show your ID, a photocopy of your passport photo page (and visa if applicable) should suffice. You may be asked to present the original document within 12 or 24 hours.

Personal Security

Although much of New Orleans is safe for visitors, there are areas, as in any city, that may not be especially tourist friendly, and things can change on a block by block basis. Use your common sense and be alert to your surroundings, and you should enjoy a trouble-free trip.

If you are mugged, do not challenge the thief. If you have anything stolen, report the crime within 24 hours to the nearest police station and take ID with you. Get a copy of the crime report in order to claim on your insurance. Contact your embassy if you have your passport stolen, or in the event of a serious crime or accident.

For emergeny police, fire, or ambulance, dial the **emergencies** number 911 free of charge from any phone. There is a different number to call for **non-emergencies**.

Hurricanes are infrequent but devastating when they do strike. The most active months for storms are August and September. If there is a storm, follow local television and radio announcements. The **National Hurricane Center** has a useful page for hurricane information and safety precautions.

As a rule, New Orleanians are very accepting of all people, regardless of their race, gender or sexuality. The city celebrates its multicultural heritage, which includes influences from French, Spanish, Cajun, Creole, German, and Indigenous communities. While New Orleans champions its LGBTQ+ communities (and was one of the first cities in the country to pass an ordinance prohibiting discrimination based on sexual orientation), the state of Louisiana remains conservative; homosexuality was only legalized in 2003 (via a Supreme Court ruling), with same-sex marriage following in 2015.

Women might experience catcalls in some parts of the French Quarter, especially around Bourbon Street, a well-known party spot.

New Orleans has a thriving LGBTQ+ scene centered on the French Quarter and Marigny. The tourism website, **Visit New Orleans**, is a useful source of information about LGBTQ+ events, bars, restaurants, hotels, and more. The Mardi Gras carnival *(see p34)*, which includes a big LGBTQ+ parade, Southern Decadence *(see p67)*, and the **Gay Easter Parade** are also major events in the city's festivals calendar.

DIRECTORY

PASSPORTS AND VISAS

ESTA
W esta.cbp.dhs.gov

U.S. Department of State
W travel.state.gov

GOVERNMENT ADVICE

Australian Department of Foreign Affairs and Trade
W dfat.gov.au
W smartraveller.gov.au

UK Foreign and Commonwealth Office
W gov.uk/foreign-travel-advice

CUSTOMS INFORMATION

U.S. Customs and Border Protection Agency
W cbp.gov/travel

HEALTH

CrescentCare
W crescentcarehealth.org

New Orleans Dental Association
W nodental.org

RiteAid
W riteaid.com

Touro Infirmary
1401 Foucher St
W touro.com

University Medical Center New Orleans
2000 Canal St
W umcno.org

Walgreens
W walgreens.com

PERSONAL SECURITY

Emergencies
T 911

Gay Easter Parade
W gayeasterparade.com

National Hurricane Center
W nhc.noaa.gov

Non-emergencies
T 504-821-2222

Visit New Orleans
W neworleans.com/things-to-do/lgbt

Travelers with Specific Requirements

Ramps, elevators, and special parking spaces can be found around the city. However, few of the historic buildings have these facilities, nor do most restaurants and bars. Always enquire about mobility restrictions in advance of visiting. Outside of the French Quarter and Downtown areas, sidewalks may be in a state of disrepair and not suitable for wheelchairs.

On public transport, both the Canal and Riverfront streetcar routes and all RTA buses have wheelchair ramps. All buses have priority seating for the elderly and those with impaired mobility. **Disability Rights Louisiana** provides advice and services for people with specific requirements. Visit New Orleans *(p113)* also has advice for getting around the city.

Time Zone

New Orleans is six hours behind Greenwich Mean Time, 17 hours behind Australia, and 19 hours behind New Zealand. DST (Daylight Saving Time) is observed from the last Sunday in March to the first Sunday in November.

Money

The official currency of the U.S. is the U.S. dollar. Most establishments in Louisiana accept major credit, debit, and prepaid currency cards. Contactless payments are becoming increasingly common, but cash is usually required by smaller shops and businesses, street vendors, and on buses.

Banks are generally open from 9am to 4pm Monday to Friday. Most New Orleans banks have ATMs outside their premises or in their lobbies. ATMs can also be found in some bars and restaurants, especially in the French Quarter. Many charge a fee.

Tipping is customary in the U.S. In restaurants it is normal to tip 15–20 per cent of the total bill. Allow for a tip of 15 per cent for taxi drivers and bar staff. Hotel porters and housekeeping expect $1–2 per bag or day.

Electrical Appliances

Electrical current flows at a voltage of 110 volts AC, and appliances require two-pronged plugs. Some non-U.S. appliances will require both a plug converter and a 110–120 volt adaptor that is compatible with the U.S. electricity system.

Cell Phones and Wi-Fi

Finding Wi-Fi hotspots is usually easy – most hotel lobbies, cafés, restaurants, bars, and public libraries offer free Wi-Fi to guests. **WiFi Map** is a handy app that finds free Wi-Fi hotspots near you.

Cell phone service in New Orleans is generally excellent. In order to use your phone abroad you may need to activate the "roaming" facility. To avoid roaming charges buy a SIM from a U.S. provider, such as **AT&T**.

Postal Services

The city's **General Post Office**, along with most other post offices, is open from 9am to 5pm Monday to Friday. Stamps can also be bought at drugstores. On-street mailboxes are usually blue, and are for letters only. Small packages must be taken to a post office.

Weather

With their temperate weather, spring and fall are the best times to visit. From May through September, the weather is hot and humid, but the city is still busy with both indoor and outdoor events. From October through March, the temperature is colder, and there are often heavy fogs. New Orleans is one of the rainiest cities in the U.S., and July and August often have showers. The hurricane season lasts from June to November, peaking in August and September.

Opening Hours

The opening hours of museums tend be from 10am to 5pm. Most stores are open from 10am to 6pm, but souvenir stores located in the French Quarter close later. Restaurants usually begin their evening service at 5pm and continue until 10pm (until 11pm on Friday and Saturday), or until the last diner leaves. Live music usually starts at 10pm, and it is a tradition that service does not stop until the last guest leaves. A number of places (attractions and restaurants) are closed on Mondays.

Many sights are closed on the following public holidays: New Year's Day (Jan 1); Martin Luther King Jr., Day (3rd Mon in Jan); President's Day (3rd Mon in Feb); Memorial Day (last Mon in May); Independence Day (Jul 4); Labor Day (Sep 2); Thanksgiving Day (Nov 28); and Christmas Day (Dec 25).

Situations can change quickly and unexpectedly. Always check before visiting attractions and hospitality venues for up-to-date opening hours and booking requirements.

Visitor Information

Visit New Orleans (p113), the official tourism website, is a useful source of information. The **New Orleans Pass** offers entry to some of the city's top sights and experiences, including museums and tours. It is available for periods of one, two, three, or five consecutive days, and can be bought online and from tourist offices.

Local Customs

Life in the city is pretty laid-back, with New Orleanians not often in a rush. Be prepared for a slower pace of life and for long chats with locals, who tend

to be unreserved and exuberantly affectionate people.

Wearing Mardi Gras beads outside of Mardi Gras season marks you as a tourist and may invite attention from pickpockets or muggers.

Language

The main language spoken in New Orleans is American English. However, Louisiana's rich cultural heritage means that a variety of languages are spoken. Words from French, Spanish, Cajun, Creole, German, and those used by Indigenous communities have also been mixed together into a New Orleans patois.

Taxes and Refunds

Taxes will be added to hotel and restaurant charges, theater tickets, some grocery and store sales, and most other purchases. Always check if tax is included in the price displayed. Sales tax is around 9 per cent, and hotel tax is around 16 per cent.

When tipping in a restaurant, it is the norm to include tax in your calculation. A quick way to calculate restaurant tips is simply to double the tax, which adds up to 18 per cent.

Tax-free shopping is available at participating stores to foreign visitors who are staying in the U.S. for fewer than 90 days. A list of the 900 or so tax-free stores and information on how to claim your refund are available on the **Louisiana Tax Free Shopping** website.

Accommodations

With around 38,000 hotel rooms available, New Orleans offers a good choice of accommodations. The city's top hotels can be expensive, but there are also many budget and mid-priced establishments, family-run B&Bs, and hostels. Hotels are busiest mid-week when business travelers are in town, and during major festivals such as Mardi Gras, when prices can more than double. It is advisable to book at least six months ahead at peak times. Rates are subject to an additional hotel tax (16 per cent), plus a $1–2 room fee per night.

DIRECTORY

TRAVELERS WITH SPECIFIC REQUIREMENTS

Disability Rights Louisiana
w disabilityrightsla.org

CELL PHONES AND WI-FI

AT&T
w att.com

Wi-Fi Map
w wifimap.io

POSTAL SERVICES

General Post Office
■ 701 Loyola Ave
w usps.com

VISITOR INFORMATION

New Orleans Pass
w neworleanspass.com

TAXES AND REFUNDS

Louisiana Tax Free Shopping
w louisiantaxfree.com

Places to Stay

PRICE CATEGORIES
For a standard double room per night during high season, including taxes and service charges.

$ under $100 $$ $100–250 $$$ over $250

Luxury Hotels

Ace Hotel New Orleans
MAP P3 ■ 600 Carondelet St ■ 504-900-1180 ■ www.acehotel.com ■ $$
The hip Ace Hotel chain debuted in the city in 2016 in this renovated historic 1928 Art Deco building. A rooftop garden, poolside dining, 234 stylish rooms, and on-site music venue, Three Keys, make this a chic choice.

AC Hotel New Orleans Bourbon
MAP N3 ■ 221 Carondelet St ■ 504-962-0700 ■ www.mariott.com/msyac ■ $$$
This stylish hotel is housed in a former 19th-century cotton trade center. The lounge has craft cocktails.

Hotel Monteleone
MAP M3 ■ 214 Royal St ■ 504-523-3341 ■ www.hotelmonteleone.com ■ $$$
The grande dame of New Orleans luxury hotels, the Monteleone (see p29) is said to be haunted, but that has not affected its popularity. It has sublime rooms, a spa, and restaurants.

International House Hotel
MAP N3 ■ 221 Camp St ■ 504-553-9550 ■ www.ihhotel.com ■ $$$
The lobby at this hotel with beautifully appointed rooms is "dressed" for summer and winter, an old New Orleans ritual. Have a drink at Loa, the hip hotel lounge (see p82).

Old No. 77 Hotel & Chandlery
MAP P4 ■ 535 Tchoupitoulas St ■ 504-527-5271 ■ www.old77hotel.com ■ $$$
The former Ambassador Hotel has been sensitively renovated into one of the city's most exciting hotels. Rooms feature hardwood floors, exposed brick, and local art, plus locally distilled rum in the mini-bar.

The Ritz-Carlton, New Orleans
MAP M3 ■ 921 Canal St ■ 504-561-0500 ■ www.ritzcarlton.com ■ $$$
This hotel (see p36), located in an artfully renovated historic building (formerly a department store) in the French Quarter, has some of the finest rooms in the city, and the service is impeccable.

The Roosevelt New Orleans
MAP N3 ■ 130 Roosevelt Way ■ 504-648-1200 ■ www.therooseveltneworleans.com ■ $$$
Gold-leaf columns decorate the lobby of this historic hotel (see p37), now part of Waldorf Astoria. The Roosevelt's legendary Blue Room, where the likes of Louis Armstrong and Ray Charles used to perform, is hired out for events.

Westin Canal Place
MAP N4 ■ 100 Iberville St ■ 504-566-7006 ■ www.westin.com ■ $$$
This hotel overlooking the Mississippi spells sheer grandeur, with an elegant dining room, a beautiful lobby with large French windows, and spacious, well-appointed rooms.

Windsor Court Hotel
MAP N4 ■ 300 Gravier St ■ 504-523-6000 ■ www.windsorcourthotel.com ■ $$$
Arguably the city's finest contemporary hotel, Windsor Court has an excellent art collection, plush rooms, and a fine-dining spot, The Grill Room.

W New Orleans – French Quarter
MAP M4 ■ 316 Chartres St ■ 504-581-1200 ■ www.wfrenchquarter.com ■ $$$
This boutique-style W has tastefully decorated rooms, an award-winning restaurant, a courtyard, and a heated outdoor pool.

Vintage Hotels

The Cornstalk Hotel
MAP L5 ■ 915 Royal St ■ 504-523-1515 ■ www.cornstalkhotel.com ■ $$
Famous for its cornstalk-shaped cast-iron fence, this charming, intimate hotel (see p28) occupies a converted 19th-century home.

Inn on St. Peter
MAP L4 ■ 1005 St. Peter St ■ 800-535-7815 ■ www.frenchquarterguesthouses.com ■ $$
In the French Quarter, Inn on St. Peter has central

courtyards and iron-lace balconies that lend it a flavor of the Old South.

Lafayette Hotel
MAP P3 ■ 600 St. Charles Ave ■ 1-888-626-5457 ■ www.thelafayettehotel.com ■ $$
Restored to its 1916 splendor, this hotel has period decor, French doors, and wrought-iron balconies. The St. Charles streetcar stops just outside.

Lamothe House Hotel
MAP K5 ■ 621 Esplanade Ave ■ 504-947-1161 ■ www.frenchquarterguesthouses.com ■ $$
This hotel provides a truly vintage New Orleans experience in a 19th-century mansion.

Le Pavillon Hotel
MAP P2 ■ 833 Poydras St ■ 504-581-3111 ■ www.lepavillon.com ■ $$
Featuring a grand lobby with high ceilings, chandeliers, and a grand dining room, this hotel has a distinct old-world charm.

Prince Conti Hotel
MAP M3 ■ 830 Conti St ■ 888-626-4319 ■ www.princecontihotel.com ■ $$
The ambience here is that of a 19th-century French chateau. Rooms are elegant, and the service is superb. The stylish Bombay Club serves Creole food.

St. James Hotel
MAP P4 ■ 330 Magazine St ■ 504-304-4000 ■ www.saintjameshotel.com ■ $$
Housed in a 19th-century former trading center, the decor of St. James reflects its Caribbean sugar and coffee trade past.

Omni Royal Orleans
MAP M4 ■ 621 St. Louis St ■ 504-529-5333 ■ www.omnihotels.com ■ $$$
This beautifully maintained French Quarter hotel (see p29) houses the fine gourmet restaurant, Rib Room.

Pontchartrain Hotel
MAP S1 ■ 2031 St. Charles Ave ■ 800-708-6652 ■ www.thepontchartrainhotel.com ■ $$$
The new incarnation of this hotel, which first opened in 1912, mixes old-world rooms with revamped public spaces, including a hip rooftop bar.

Royal Sonesta Hotel
MAP M4 ■ 300 Bourbon St ■ 504-586-0300 ■ www.royalsonesta.com ■ $$$
The elegant Royal Sonesta (see p33) combines a rich heritage with modern amenities. It is home to The Jazz Playhouse.

Soniat House
MAP L5 ■ 133 Chartres St ■ 504-522-0570 ■ www.soniathouse.com ■ $$$
Built in 1829, Soniat House has the intimacy of a private home. Rooms are individually decorated with attention to details. The hotel is a favorite with celebrities.

Business Hotels

Hilton Garden Inn – New Orleans Convention Center
MAP R4 ■ 1001 S. Peters St ■ 504-525-0044 ■ www.hiltongardeninn3.hilton.com ■ $$
Just across from the Ernest N. Morial Convention Center, this modern property has a relaxed ambience and an American restaurant.

Hilton Riverside Hotel
MAP P4 ■ 2 Poydras St ■ 504-561-0500 ■ www.hilton.com ■ $$
Located on the banks of the Mississippi, this large hotel is a favorite with business travelers heading to the nearby Ernest N. Morial Convention Center.

Hyatt French Quarter
MAP L2 ■ 800 Iberville St ■ 504-586-0800 ■ www.frenchquarter.hyatt.com ■ $$
Spacious rooms have clean design touches and high ceilings. Guests can enjoy the outdoor pool area and cocktails at the hotel bar.

Le Méridien New Orleans
MAP P2 ■ 333 Poydras St ■ 504-525-9444 ■ www.lemeridienneworleanshotel.com ■ $$
This former W hotel has been redesigned with an emphasis on contemporary decor influenced by New Orleans culture.

Sheraton New Orleans Hotel
MAP N4 ■ 500 Canal St ■ 504-525-2500 ■ www.sheratonneworleans.com ■ $$
Spacious rooms, modern amenities, and a central location ensure a loyal clientele. There are five majestic ballrooms and 54 meeting rooms.

Hotel Inter-Continental
MAP N3 ■ 444 St. Charles Ave ■ 504-525-5566 ■ www.ichotelsgroup.com ■ $$$
Large rooms with modern workspace accessories make this hotel popular with business travelers.

Hyatt Regency New Orleans

MAP P2 ▪ 601 Loyola Ave ▪ 504-561-1234 ▪ www.neworleans. hyatt.com ▪ $$$
This vast hotel overlooking the Caesars Superdome (see p80) has an extensive meeting and exhibition space.

Loews Hotel

MAP P4 ▪ 300 Poydras St ▪ 504-595-3300 ▪ www. loewshotels.com ▪ $$$
No expense has been spared on the furnishings, lighting, and art adorning this hotel, with some of the largest rooms in the city.

Renaissance Pere Marquette

MAP N3 ▪ 817 Common St ▪ 504-525-1111 ▪ www.marriott.com ▪ $$$
This historic downtown hotel has been renovated into a luxurious property with stylish decor.

Windsor Court Hotel

MAP P4 ▪ 300 Gravier St ▪ 800-262-2662 ▪ www. windsorcourthotel.com ▪ $$$
The luxurious Windsor Court Hotel offers spacious, state-of-the-art rooms with great views and an outdoor pool.

Mid-Range Hotels

Aloft New Orleans Downtown

MAP N3 ▪ 225 Baronne St ▪ 504-581-9225 ▪ www. marriott.com ▪ $$
The 188 loft-style rooms are minimalist but chic, with plush bedding and upscale amenities. The fitness center, outdoor pool, and neon-lit W XYZ lobby bar make this hotel great value.

Club Wyndham Avenue Plaza

MAP J4 ▪ 2111 St. Charles Ave ▪ 504-566-1212 ▪ https://clubwyndham. wyndhamdestinations. com ▪ $$
This all-suite hotel bills itself as a resort with a swimming pool. All rooms have an old-world charm and their own kitchenettes.

Blake Hotel

MAP P3 ▪ 500 St. Charles Ave ▪ 504-522-9000 ▪ www.blakehotelnew orleans.com ▪ $$
The finely renovated Blake Hotel is a short walk from the riverfront and the St. Charles streetcar. The on-site restaurant Café at the Square offers great weekend brunches.

Bon Maison Guest House

MAP L4 ▪ 835 Bourbon St ▪ 504-561-8498 ▪ $$
This 19th-century townhouse, located in the French Quarter, has been refashioned into a guesthouse built around a beautiful courtyard.

Catahoula Hotel

MAP N2 ▪ 914 Union St ▪ 504-603-2442 ▪ www. selina.com/usa/catahoula-new-orleans ▪ $$
Set in a charmingly restored 1845 Creole townhouse, this chic hotel has modern furnishings with Peruvian accents. There's a lovely rooftop terrace, a café serving Latin-inspired fare, and the Pisco Bar.

Columns Hotel

MAP C6 ▪ 3811 St. Charles Ave ▪ 504-899-9308 ▪ www.thecolumns. com ▪ $$
Relaxing with a cocktail on the Columns' front porch is an ideal way to start your holiday at this Italianate building designed in 1883 by New Orleans architect, Thomas Sully. The rooms are a little old-fashioned, but the moderate pricing makes it worthwhile.

Dauphine Orleans Hotel

MAP M3 ▪ 415 Dauphine St ▪ 504-586-1800 ▪ www. dauphineorleans. com ▪ $$
This French Quarter hotel includes a number of 19th-century buildings that were inhabited by the artist John James Audubon. Rooms are modern, and there's complimentary breakfast and Wi-Fi, plus an outdoor saltwater pool.

Hotel Le Marais

MAP M3 ▪ 717 Conti St ▪ 504-525-2300 ▪ www. hotellemarais.com ▪ $$
A modern addition to a historic district, Le Marais is half a block from Bourbon Street, right in the thick of the action. The courtyard offers a welcome respite, and the heated saltwater pool is lovely. The interior design is striking, with bold, chic colors, and there is also a good complimentary continental breakfast.

Hotel Mazarin

MAP M3 ▪ 730 Bienville St ▪ 504-581-7300 ▪ www. hotelmazarin.com ▪ $$
Set back from the bustle of Bourbon Street, this hotel has 102 rooms that feature black granite bathrooms and high-end cotton bedding. The attached wine bar is a nice amenity, and the complimentary breakfast is wonderful.

Moxy New Orleans Downtown

MAP N2 ▪ 210 O'Keefe Ave ▪ 504-525-6800 ▪ www. marriott.com ▪ $$
This spirited, vibrant boutique hotel is near the French Quarter. Modern touches include 24/7 self-service nibbles, a popular cocktail bar, and free high-speed Internet.

The Whitney Hotel

MAP N1 ▪ 610 Poydras Str ▪ 504-581-4222 ▪ www.whitneyhotel. com ▪ $$
The architecture of this hotel, in a former bank in the CBD, gives it a novel feel. The original vault is a notable feature, as are the brass fittings, and crown moldings. The traditionally decorated rooms are extremely quiet thanks to the property's thick walls.

St. Charles Inn

MAP C6 ▪ 3636 St. Charles Ave ▪ 504-899-8888 ▪ www.stcharles inn.com ▪ $$$
The clean and comfortable St. Charles Inn is set in a busy part of town dotted with good restaurants. The streetcar stops right outside, providing access to most city attractions.

Bed and Breakfast

Ashton's Bed & Breakfast

MAP E2 ▪ 2023 Esplanade Ave ▪ 504-942-7048 ▪ www.ashtonsbb.com ▪ $$
Lovingly transformed into a bed and breakfast, this Greek revival mansion has a main house featuring high ceilings, spacious rooms, and some fine period furnishings.

Chimes Bed & Breakfast

MAP C6 ▪ 1146 Constantinople St ▪ 504-899-2621 ▪ www.chimes neworleans.com ▪ $$
This uptown inn oozes historic charm. Each of the five rooms has its own private entrance and French doors opening onto a common courtyard.

Dauphine House

MAP K5 ▪ 1830 Dauphine St ▪ 504-940-0943 ▪ www. dauphinehouse.com ▪ $$
Built in 1860, Dauphine House has high ceilings and hardwood floors, and is just around the corner from the French Quarter. For most months of the year some rooms are available for under $100.

Degas House

MAP E2 ▪ 2306 Esplanade Ave ▪ 504-821-5009 ▪ www.degashouse.com ▪ $$
French Impressionist Edgar Degas stayed and painted in this house (see p104) on a picturesque street. It is now a well-kept bed and breakfast.

Elysian Fields Inn

MAP K6 ▪ 930 Elysian Fields Ave ▪ 504-948-9420 ▪ www.elysianfields inn.com ▪ $$
This charming B&B sits within walking distance to the music scene on Frenchmen St. It has a shaded back porch, a refreshingly green back-yard, and stately rooms.

Lafitte Guest House

MAP L4 ▪ 1003 Bourbon St ▪ 504-581-2678 ▪ www.lafitteguest house.com ▪ $$
A restored 19th-century property in the heart of the French Quarter, this guesthouse is richly decorated and has rooms filled with antiques and a quiet courtyard.

Maison Perrier Bed & Breakfast

MAP C6 ▪ 4117 Perrier St ▪ 504-897-1807 ▪ www. maisonperrier.com ▪ $$
This grand home was built in 1892 and is a nationally registered historic place. It has a lovely library, elegant sitting rooms and charming sleeping quarters with Victorian-style decorative accents.

Melrose Mansion

MAP K5 ▪ 937 Esplanade Ave ▪ MAP K5 ▪ 504-944-2255 ▪ www.melrose mansion.com ▪ $$
Set in a huge Victorian Gothic-style mansion built in 1884, this luxurious bed-and-breakfast is imbued with old-world charm. It features one of the most romantic suites in the city.

Sully Mansion

MAP H5 ▪ 631 Prytania St ▪ 504-891-0457 ▪ $$
Designed in 1890 by local architect Thomas Sully, this mansion has a lovely wraparound porch. It has just nine guest rooms and is quite close to the St. Charles streetcar line.

The Henry Howard Hotel

MAP J4 ▪ 2041 Prytania St ▪ 504-313-1577 ▪ www.henryhoward hotel.com ▪ $$$
Named for the man who built this mansion in 1867, this hotel is an elegant blend of traditional vintage furniture and modern amenities. The Parlor is a splendid setting to sip a craft cocktail.

General Index

Acknowledgments

This edition updated by

Contributor Adam Karlin

Senior Editors Dipika Dasgupta, Alison McGill

Senior Art Editor Vinita Venugopal

Project Editor Anuroop Sanwalia

Project Art Editor Bharti Karakoti

Editor Charlie Baker

Assistant Editor Tavleen Kaur

Picture Research Administrator Vagisha Pushp

Picture Research Manager Taiyaba Khatoon

Publishing Assistant Simona Velikova

Jacket Designer Jordan Lambley

Senior Cartographer Subhashree Bharati

Cartography Manager Suresh Kumar

DTP Designer Rohit Rojal

Senior Production Editor Jason Little

Production Controller Kariss Ainsworth

Managing Editors Shikha Kulkarni,
Beverly Smart, Hollie Teague

Managing Art Editor Sarah Snelling

Senior Managing Art Editor Priyanka Thakur

Art Director Maxine Pedliham

Publishing Director Georgina Dee

DK would like to thank the following
for their contribution to the previous editions:
Hilary Bird, Ella Buchan, Paul Greenberg,
Paul Oswell, Clare Peele, Helena Smith,
Greg Ward, Stuart West

The publisher would like to thank the
following for their kind permission to
reproduce their photographs:

Key: a-above; b-below/bottom; c-center; f-far;
l-left; r-right; t-top

123RF.com: legacy1995 92bl.

Alamy Stock Photo: Irene Abdou 16-7, 17br,
81bl; age fotostock / Judie Long 43cl; Ann Ronan
Picture Library / Photo12 40br; Carol Barrington
18cla; Charles O. Cecil 36cla, 82tl, 88cl, 100t;
Ian Dagnall 58bl, 73crb, 91tl; Danita Delimont /
Jamie & Judy Wild 10cl; GJGK Photography 42tl;
Tim Graham 69tr, 93tl; Spencer Grant 46crb, 96cl;
hemis.fr / Patrick Frilet 11bl; Robert Holmes 21tr,
38-9; James Houser New Orleans 98-9, 104-5;
Images-USA 62br; incamerastock 33br; Keystone
Press / Keystone Pictures USA 41cla; Russell
Kord 11tr; Jason Langley 12-3c; Simon Leigh 61tr;
Lifestyle pictures / Will Packer Productions / Perfect
World Pictures 51br; Ninette Maumus 7tc, 16cl;
Nikreates 75cl; James Quine 23tr; Reuters / Sean
Gardner 64b; RM USA 74tl; RosaBetancourt 0
people images 63tr; Philip Scalia 34-5; Spia US
42br; Travel Pictures / Pictures Colour Library
4cla; UPI 41br; WWPics / Matthew D. White 34cl;
Jim West 102cl; Jennifer Wright 36-7; ZUMAPRESS.
com / Dan Anderson 35tr; ZUMA Press, Inc. 66tr.

Arnaud's: 60cb, 94ca.

Audubon Nature Institute: 73t; Audubon Zoo
Jeff Strout 10clb, 10crb, 48bl.

August: Randy Schmidt 85cb.

BB's Stage Door Canteen: 50cla.

Bridgeman Images: The Historic New Orleans
Collection / Acquisition from the Clarisse Claiborne
Grima Fund 40tl.

Café Degas: 107b.

Café Lafittes: 55cra.

Café NOMA by Ralph Brennan: 13tl.

Cole Pratt Gallery: J. Stephen Young 76tl.

Commander's Palace: 60t.

Courtesy of Arthur Roger Gallery: *Hell Hell Hell
Heaven Heaven Heaven: Encountering Sister Gertrude
Morgan & Revelation* Lesley Dill October 2010
Exhibition 83bl.

Delmonico: 57ca.

Dreamstime.com: Amadeustx 74b; Bhofack2 56tr,
57tr; Tony Bosse 79br; Emilysfolio 27c; F11photo
11clb, 33tr, 65tr; Fotoluminate 29cr; Giban59 69cla;
Jorg Hackemann 3tr, 22bl, 28-9, 108-9; Imagecom
4t; Imagecom 26bc; Wangkun Jia 49t; Olivier Le
Queinec 4cra; Erik Lattwein 10clb; Legacy1995 4b;
Chon Kit Leong 11cra; Maomaotou 4r; Sean Pavone
2tl, 3tl, 8-9, 26-7, 32-3, 68t, 70-1, 90b; Ppy2010ha
56cb; Kevin Ruck 6cla; Anthony Aneese Totah Jr
98clb; Typhoonski 63cl; Lawrence Weslowski Jr 10b,
32cl.

Emeril's: J. Stephen Young 77cr.

LeMieux Galleries: *Contact Tracing* (2015), Aron Belka
80 x 80 inches, oil on canvas / Aron Belka 83cra.

Getty Images: AFP / Robyn Beck 35bc; Bloomberg /
Bryan Tarnowski 46tl; FilmMagic / Eric Isaacs 28bl;
Erika Goldring 53tr, 53cl, 64tc; Tim Graham 106tr;
Kylie McLaughlin 97tr; Redferns / Leon Morris 52bl;
Paul Rovere 31b; Stone / Peter Unger 1; The Image
Bank Unreleased / Atlantide Phototravel 18-19ca;
UIG / Education Images 36bl, 62tl; WireImage /
Josh Brasted 94b.

Halloween New Orleans: 67tr.

The Historic New Orleans Collection: 20cla, 20bl,
20-21ca, 21tl, 45cr, 90ca.

Howlin' Wolf: 52t.

Getty Images/iStock: Ampueroleonardo 43tr; holgs
23crb; Jfbenning 37tl; JHVE Photo 80t; krblokhin
101clb; Gregory Kurpiel 86-7; mixmotive 22-3c;
Pgiam 7cr; SeanPavonePhoto 24-5; Sfe-Co2 65cl;
TerryJ 72cl.

Louisiana State Museum: Mark J. Sindler
26cla, 49br.

Marigny Opera House: Pompo Bresciani 99bl.

Maskarade: Lisa Negrotto 93c.

Mother's Restaurant: 59br.

Napoleon House: Chris Granger 95cr.

Courtesy of The National WWII Museum: 10crb,
18br, 19tr, 44b.

**Courtesy of the New Orleans Museum of Art Photos
by Roman Alokhin and Judy Cooper:** 12clb; *Portrait of
Mrs. Asher B. Wertheimer*, 1898, John Singer Sargent,
Oil on canvas, purchase in memory of William H.
Henderson, 78.3 10ca; *Madonna and Child with Saints*,

circa 1340, Benvenuto di Giovanni (follower of),
Tempera on wood, The Samuel H. Kress Collection,
61.60 14t; *Kwakiutl, Dance Apron,* circa early 20th
century, Unidentified, fabrics, glass beads, brass
bells, Gift of an Anonymous Donor, 94.214 14cb;
Portrait of Marie Antoinette, Queen of France, circa
1788, Elisabeth Louise Vigeé Le Brun, Oil on canvas,
Museum purchase, Women's Volunteer Committee
and Carrie Heiderich Fund, 85.90 15bl; *Unique Forms
of Continuity in Space.* 1913 (cast 1931) Umberto
Boccioni 103bc; *LOVE, Red Blue,* 1966-1997, Robert
Indiana, Aluminum with acrylic polyurethane enamel,
72 x 72 x 36 in.; 182.88 x 182.88 x 91.44 cm, Museum
purchase, Sydney and Walda Besthoff Foundation,
2004.119 photo Richard Sexton © Morgan Art
Foundation Ltd. / Artists Rights Society (ARS),
New York, DACS, London 2017 13br.

New Orleans City Park Archives: 4l, 17tc, 48cr,
103t, 105cl.

New Orleans Pharmacy Museum: 47tr

New Orleans Wine & Food Experience (NOWFE):
Chris Granger 66b.

courtesy Ogden Museum of Southern Art: *Me, Knife,
Diamond and Flower* by James Surls, photo Carroll
Grevemberg 80clb.

The Outlet Collection at Riverwalk: 84b.

OZ: 54clb.

Palace Café: Sara Essex Bradley 85cla.

Photoshot: LOOK 69b.

Robert Harding Picture Library: Tim Graham 79t.

The Rodrigue Studio: George Rodrigue 29b.

Satchmo Summer Fest: Zack Smith Photography 67cl.

Shaya: 61bl.

Shutterstock.com: JustPixs 81cl; Theresa
Launia 11crb.

Southern Food & Beverage Museum: 45tl

SuperStock: Seth Resnick 89t.

The Saenger Theatre: 50b.

Trashy Diva: Brittney Werner 62c.

Villa Vici: 76bc.

Cover

Front and spine: **Getty Images:** Stone / Peter Unger
Back: **Dreamstime.com:** Exposurestonature cla,
Meinzahn tl, Sean Pavone crb, tr; **Getty Images:**
Stone / Peter Unger b

Pull Out Map Cover

Getty Images: Stone / Peter Unger

All other images are © Dorling Kindersley
For further information see: www.dkimages.com

Penguin
Random
House

First edition 2010

Published in Great Britain by
Dorling Kindersley Limited,
DK, One Embassy Gardens, 8 Viaduct
Gardens, London SW11 7BW, UK

The authorised representative in the EEA is
Dorling Kindersley Verlag GmbH. Arnulfstr.
124, 80636 Munich, Germany

Published in the United States by
DK Publishing, 1745 Broadway, 20th Floor,
New York, NY 10019, USA

Copyright © 2010, 2024
Dorling Kindersley Limited
A Penguin Random House Company

23 24 25 26 10 9 8 7 6 5 4 3 2 1

A CIP catalog record is available
from the British Library.

A catalog record for this book is available
from the Library of Congress.

ISSN 1479-344X

ISBN 978-0-2416-6267-0

Print and bound in Malaysia

www.dk.com

*As a guide to abbreviations in visitor information
blocks:* **Adm** = admission charge; **L** = lunch;
D = dinner.

MIX
Paper | Supporting
responsible forestry
FSC™ C018179

This book was made with Forest
Stewardship Council™ certified
paper – one small step in DK's
commitment to a sustainable future.
**For more information go to
www.dk.com/our-green-pledge**

Street Index